PRAISE FOR
SLAY LIKE A MOTHER

"Entertaining and honest, Katherine's story reveals that the most powerful force for changing your life is you."
—Mel Robbins, author of the international bestseller *The 5 Second Rule*

"*Life-changing.* That is the only way to summarize the impact of *Slay Like a Mother*. As I devoured the transformative words of this book, I wished I'd had it during a desolate time in my life—but it was not too late. Every time fear, anxiety, inadequacy, or self-doubt gripped me, I opened *Slay Like a Mother*. Waiting to inspire me was a relatable anecdote or foolproof strategy with the power to help me say no, draw a boundary line, ask for help, and show up for my life. *Slay Like a Mother* is much more than a self-help book for women; it is the end of self-doubt and the beginning of self-love…and *that* is nothing short of life-changing."
—Rachel Macy Stafford, *New York Times* bestselling author of *Hand Free Mama, Hands Free Life*, and *Only Love Today*

"*Slay Like a Mother* is a feisty, clever, and fun blueprint for modern motherhood that belongs on every bookshelf and in every diaper bag. No mom has time for a drippy self-help tome, and this guide cuts right to the point: when you turn your doubt into strength, the sky's the limit. As a woman and mother, you'll gain a newfound power, happiness, and ability to leap tall Lego buildings in a single bound."
—Erin Falconer, author of *How to Get Sh*t Done: Why Women Need to Stop Doing Everything So They Can Achieve Anything*

"I love everything about this book. The tone, the candor, the acceptance that we must love ourselves first before we can slay anything in life. And it is so needed. We mothers are experts at thinking we are not good enough or do enough. It is time for us to let go of the guilt and let in the love. Thank you for this gift, Katherine. Slay on!"

—Julie Foudy, former captain of the U.S. women's national soccer team, ESPN analyst and reporter, and Olympic gold medalist

"In a world where the highlight reels of social media have set the perfect standard for what's expected in motherhood, *Slay Like a Mother* is the much-needed antidote for imperfect moms who feel like they're always falling short. This book leads you back to yourself with kind guidance you would get from your best girlfriend and practical exercises you could expect from your favorite therapist. Every woman and mother needs this book!"

—Kathleen Shannon, cofounder of branding agency Braid Creative, host of the *Being Boss* podcast, and author of *Being Boss: Take Control of Your Work and Live Life on Your Terms*

"*Slay Like a Mother* spoke to my heart! I felt this book was meant for me and meant for so many other moms I know. This book reaches into the depths of yourself and helps you discover where your self-doubt started, how it manifested, and fantastic tools to slay that inner beast! This is a must-read, not just for moms, but for anyone struggling with self-doubt."

—Dana Vollmer, five-time Olympic gold medalist, first mom to win Olympic gold for USA in swimming

Slay

LIKE A

MOTHER

HOW TO DESTROY
WHAT'S HOLDING YOU BACK SO
YOU CAN *Live the Life You Want*

KATHERINE WINTSCH

sourcebooks

To my husband, Richard.

While many have been able to see a light within me that I couldn't see myself, you were the first to recognize that I couldn't see it. Thank you for encouraging me to develop the love, respect, and self-compassion I needed to thrive and help others do the same. We make one heck of a team.

Published by Sourcebooks
P.O. Box 4410, Naperville, Illinois 60567-4410
(630) 961-3900
Fax: (630) 961-2168
sourcebooks.com

Library of Congress Cataloging-in-Publication Data is on file with the publisher.

Printed and bound in the United States of America.
VP 10 9 8 7 6 5 4

Contents

PART III: GETTING RID OF YOUR DRAGON FOR GOOD

Slay On

Welcome to an exciting journey of personal growth and development. Throughout this book you'll be prompted to answer thought-provoking questions about your past, present, and future. Feel free to write your answers directly in the book or visit slaylikeamother.com to download a PDF version of the exercises.

Invitation

The dragon raging inside you has a name, and it's self-doubt.
You're the only one who can see it, so you're the only one who can slay it.

You have two choices. You either learn to slay
this beast, or it will slowly and silently slay you.

If you don't rise up and take back your life and sanity,
the constant battle and fighting will wear you down and
wear you out. And you, your family, and the world will miss
out on the best of you.

You already have all the tools, resources, and weapons you need
within you to slay this dragon. You just don't know it because
you've been denying the dragon's existence for entirely too long.

I slayed my dragon, and my life dramatically improved.
Now, I've dedicated my life to helping other women do
the same. You can do this. I will help you.

Let's go slay some dragons!

INTRODUCTION

Come Slay with Me

Are you tired of working your ass off and *still* feeling like you should be doing more?

Does the negative voice in your head constantly mouth off to the tune "When are you going to get your act together, lady?" Do other mothers seem to glide through life on ice skates while you tuck your muffin top into your pants and pray you'll make it through Tuesday without losing your ever-loving mind?

If so, you picked up the right book.

The time has come to embark on the next chapter of your life—away from the illusion that you're never doing enough and toward the deeply held belief that you've always been more than enough. Navigating this messy world as a human, woman, and mother is not easy. That's a fact. However, much to your horror but soon your relief, I have ten years of research and twenty years of personal experiences (ahem, mistakes) that indicate you might be making life a lot harder than it has to be. Yes, I just said that, and it's time for you to believe it.

It's easy to blame your micromanaging boss, the hyperactive PTA president, your son's teenage antics, or your partner's missing sensitivity chip for the stress and pressure that's been building for years, but they're not the root cause. The demands of a busy life are taxing, but they don't exhaust your soul. It's the warped belief that you can and should be doing more that's keeping you down.

How do I know? Because I was a card-carrying member of that club for years. From the time I was a teenager to well after I gave birth, I suffered at the hands of my own unrealistic expectations, inability to say no, and relentless pursuit of making my life appear as though it was under control. To glance at the trappings of success in my life—the titles, the trophies, the *Today* show appearances—you might assume I was always free from the nagging doubts and fears that torment so many women, especially mothers, around the world. But there's more to my story than superficial achievements. If you look beneath the surface and beyond the optical delusions that blindly impress most people, you'll find a very different narrative, one I'm not embarrassed but proud to share with you in hopes it sparks your own heroic journey toward eradicating what's holding you back.

I spent two decades collecting external signs of success, not because I wanted to fill the empty spaces on my bookshelf, but because I needed to fill a hole inside me. (Spoiler alert: there's a difference.) My emptiness stemmed from feeling less than for the majority of my life. And while my world looked firmly pressed and buttoned-up on the outside, I was always running, always chasing, rarely satisfied, and I never felt good enough. But I silenced my struggles and, as a result, handed my strength and self-worth to a dragon that raged inside me.

Perhaps you've done the same.

WHAT'S IN A DRAGON?

I like to refer to our self-defeating tendencies as our "dragons" for two reasons. First, when you're fighting against your own self-doubt, it feels like a never-ending, always exhausting battle is being waged inside you. Operating from a deficit in the self-love department forces you to feel as if you must fight, protect, battle, defend, and claw your way to the top of other people's opinions, and you become tired because of it. Second, self-doubt is a beast. It feels bigger, bolder, and braver than your fragile ego, and its weapon of choice is to inhale everything you're doing wrong and nothing you're doing right and blow it back in your face.

The time has come to slay what's holding you back, because while questioning whether you're smart enough, pretty enough, nice enough, or mom enough on a daily basis probably feels normal to you, it's not healthy. Once you find the courage to kick your dragon to the curb, you'll find freedom in the fact that life doesn't have to be *this* hard. Soon, you'll see that dealing with the chaos around you becomes light-years easier when you're not fighting chaos within you.

FACING THE TRUTH

When I was eight years old, I overheard my father describe me to one of his friends. "My daughter is like a cat," he said. "She's calm and cuddly until she gets backed into a corner. That's when the claws come out." His description felt accurate at the time, and I'm not going to lie:

I kind of liked it. The metaphor continued to play out as I got older, but nowhere did it feature more prominently than in my battle to love, trust, and believe in myself as a woman and mother.

When I played host mom to my dragon, I lived as a muted version of myself—biting my tongue and holding my breath as I allowed external approval, affection, and accolades to determine my self-worth. Finally, the day came when I realized that so much performing, perfecting, and pleasing was no way to live. I wanted out. I'd been backed into a corner by my archenemy, and after some serious soul searching, I slayed the hell out of that beast and never looked back.

So how did I finally find the courage to turn my self-doubt into self-compassion and eventually empowerment? Just when I was at my lowest of lows, in 2010, the stars aligned for me to conduct a research study with an international sample of mothers to help pitch and win the global Johnson & Johnson business in my role as a senior vice president at a national advertising agency. I threw traditional (and boring) research methodologies such as focus groups out the window, because I'd been frustrated for years watching mothers in such groups pass themselves off as perfect in an attempt to look good in front of the other mothers in the room. Instead, I asked mothers from Shanghai to Seattle to document and discuss their deepest doubts and proudest accomplishments, their greatest wishes and regrets, and their tips for navigating the messy world of modern motherhood. In the end, we didn't win the account, but I won the lottery. I uncovered the truth about what happens inside the minds of moms, and that truth set me free. Now, I want to set you free as well.

I'll share some of this research throughout this book because I believe the insights and stories will provide as much relief to you as they did to me. Simply knowing I wasn't alone was the spark I needed to set off a two-year self-help journey during which I read, studied, evaluated, and tested advice from spiritual gurus, TV talk show hosts, meditation teachers, and other mothers. That is to say, I took one for the team: I did the hard work necessary to discover why some moms are holding themselves back—and how we can all free ourselves from the guilt and pain that ensues. The insight, tools, and advice I collected and applied to my own life changed *everything*. I went from broken to whole, from silent to vocal, from embarrassed to proud. Ever since, I've hosted workshops and seminars for moms across the country who feel as defeated as I once did. Moms of every kind attend—working, stay-at-home, married, divorced, urban, suburban, gay, straight—all of whom are desperate to heal and thrive.

YOU'RE NOT ALONE

Though I initially assumed I was the only mother annihilating myself for not being and doing more, discovering that millions—yes, millions!—of other moms also fought their own manipulative, fire-breathing, anxiety-provoking dragons offered me tremendous relief and freedom. If you're fighting this battle, take heart because (1) so are legions of other women around the globe and (2) this doesn't mean you're stupid, oversensitive, inadequate, or a loser. In fact, there's a very noticeable method to your madness. A clear exchange—a kind of cause and effect—occurs in your psyche that urges you to work overtime. Basically, you don't feel good enough most of the time, so you strive to be seen as more than enough *all* the time to make up the difference. The imbalance leaves you feeling destabilized.

My goal is to help you realize that you are already *more than enough* as a mother and as a woman. Not only were you born with exactly what you need to live a life free from fear and filled with inner peace, but you also deserve it. Every mother deserves to feel a sense of pride and relief when she lays her head on the pillow at the end of an exhaustingly long day, and you are no exception to that rule. There is a beautiful soul inside you that deserves to be valued, trusted, and celebrated at every turn, and I'll help you to take the courageous steps necessary to get there. You'll quickly realize that, with the right tools, insight, and encouragement, you can slay your self-doubting dragon and live a happier, more peaceful existence.

You've got this, Mama.

HOW TO USE THIS BOOK

I wrote *Slay Like a Mother* for self-doubting mothers like me—like us. If you've picked up this book, it's because not feeling good enough as a woman has turned into not feeling good enough as a mom, and you're ready to deal with these feelings, once and for all. Be prepared to learn that you're not alone and accept that you're capable of conquering your inner beast.

Here's how it will go down. I'll take you on a four-part journey that moves you away from fear and toward freedom. I'll combine compelling research with practical tips I've used in my life and learned from dragon-slaying moms who have transformed their own sense of self so that you can begin to leave unhelpful patterns behind. I'll begin by sharing my own trials and how I tamed and slayed my dragon, plus differentiate between the struggling and suffering that moms undergo to help you grasp what's going on. This foundation will help you—as it's helped hundreds of women in my workshops—begin to acknowledge and evaluate your own dragon of self-doubt, including the collateral damage it has caused. In part 2, I'll explore the seven ways you're feeding your dragon, such as setting expectations that are too high, yelling at yourself all day long, and fearing the worst for the future. In part 3, I'll teach you how to use honesty, self-respect, and self-love to get rid of your dragon for good. And in part 4, you'll recognize, appreciate, and make the most of a life free of friction and embrace the positive ripple effect it has on others, including your newfound ability to pass inner peace on to your children.

After reading *Slay Like a Mother*, you'll have a better understanding of what you're fighting, why it's such an excruciating battle, and how to achieve a sense of calm and happiness that will impact everyone around you. It's time for this exhausting battle to go from dark, quiet, and embarrassing to bold, public, and prideful. Struggling in silence yields shame; struggling out loud breeds courage.

Every great accomplishment begins with the courage to try. Mine did and yours will too.

PART I

LET'S
Slay
TOGETHER

CHAPTER 1

Fighting and Winning My Own Battle

*B*efore we get into the blood and guts of how to beat down your dragon, I'd like to share my own journey so you can trace how I arrived where I am today. This might help you better understand why your dragon has been able to thrive for so long. Though our lives are not identical, I do suspect there are similar themes that will feel familiar and lend you both insight and inspiration that you, too, will soon be on the other side of this fight. My ultimate hope is that my journey from broken to whole will inspire you to bring your own truth out of the darkness and into the light.

Here we go.

Growing up, I was loved. But unlike my older brother, Chris, I couldn't always see it. He and I were born into a family blessed with strong marriages, successful careers, and pull-yourself-up-by-your-bootstraps characters. Our childhood was filled with happiness, and the signs were everywhere—beach vacations with aunts, uncles, grand-parents, and cousins; annual ski trips; weekends waterskiing at our river house; late-night chats on the front porch; sleepovers on the backyard trampoline; and family spaghetti dinners on the regular. Our house was *the house* where everyone wanted to hang out because the life, energy, and vibe was *that* intoxicating. Once you got a taste of it, you didn't want to leave. My parents made life, marriage, and happiness look effortless, which was a joy for them and anyone who spent time in their company.

As early as ten years old, I sensed I was born with an extra dose of sensitivity that I didn't see in others, and it affected how I experienced and processed everything around me. I was particularly sensitive to pain—both mine and others'—and tried to avoid it at all cost. When I saw a homeless man for the first time and sensed his physical pain from living on the frigid streets in the dead of winter, I took all my crumpled dollar bills to the closest Salvation Army to see how many winter coats I could buy for those like him. In the fourth grade, when a boy named Jacob asked me to be his girlfriend by checking yes or no on the note he passed me, I didn't want to hurt his feelings by saying no, so I politely returned the note and suggested he send it to Angela, one of our classmates who had a crush on him—she was sure to say yes! And when my brother and I were punished for our childhood antics, I could see it frustrated him, while the exact same punishment *devastated* me—my parents' disappointment seemed to cut me harder, hurt me more, and stuck to me like glue that was impossible to wash off.

Research by clinical psychologist Dr. Elaine Aron indicates that roughly 20 percent of the population is affected by sensory processing sensitivity (SPS), an innate trait associated with greater sensitivity, or responsiveness, to environmental and social stimuli. In other words, their brains take in more information, process it more deeply, and become overstimulated and easily overwhelmed. Biologists have also discovered this trait in over one hundred species, from fruit flies, birds, and fish to horses, cats, dogs, and primates. Never thought you'd have anything in common with a fruit fly, huh? Apparently, a heightened level of sensitivity reflects a kind of survival strategy that makes you feel the need to be overly observant before acting. This trait makes all the sense in the world to me because it's how I managed my life as a child in order to avoid pain; I would observe what mattered most to the people around me and go after it with gusto.

My parents loved to feel and spread happiness, and they seemed happiest when my brother and I made them proud. Difficult topics or situations were not discussed in my house, as my parents preferred to avoid the bad and talk about the good. So my brother and I made sure to give them a lot of good things to talk about. As a result, they showered us with love notes when we completed our chores without being asked, cheered loudly on the sidelines of sporting events, and worked closely with us during poster-making parties when we ran for president of the Student Council Association. You can only imagine how good it felt, then, when I was elected president of my elementary school in fifth grade. I ran a killer campaign; the race wasn't even close. My parents didn't like losing, and they certainly weren't going to lose to a bunch of fifth graders! Our family seemed destined to achieve great things—that same year, I solidified my place in our collective success story when my name was inscribed on a brick sidewalk in downtown Richmond, Virginia, where I grew up. I was featured in the local newspaper as an outstanding student, and I was praised by everyone who knew my family. I liked the way recognition felt. It felt like love, and I wanted more of it.

Perfection was an undeniable currency in my house. You name it, and my parents perfected it—pressed hospital corners on every bed, screwdrivers hung in descending sizes so a missing one was immediately noticeable, and my own bedroom in which nothing was allowed on the wall without being properly framed, measured, and hung in the right place. I was perceptive as a child, but that skill wasn't necessary here. I could have been blind and still noticed that an unerring nature and attention to detail meant a lot to my parents.

As a kid, I found these tendencies to be highly annoying, though I played along. Submitting to a room check before going to a sleepover or spending three hours on a Saturday picking up pinecones in the backyard was not something I saw happening at my friends' houses. However, the successful lives I was told these habits led to also didn't seem to happen at my friends' houses. So, as my family walked the walk, I learned that the end game of perfection was success, and this kept me in line. I put my back into mirroring the behaviors I saw around me.

When your father models that you can have a high-powered corporate career without moving to a big city, your mother manages to juggle being a great parent and having a successful career as a nurse, and your big brother dedicates his life to public service as a battalion chief in the fire department? Well, let's just say it's a good idea to keep your shit together. And I did, for a long time. By the end of middle school, my picture-perfect room was overrun with proof of accomplishments—swim team ribbons, physical fitness awards, soccer pins, gymnastics medals, press releases from skiing competitions, excellence in academics certificates, and straight-A report cards, all properly framed for the world to see. Being a good girl was an easy way for me to please multiple people at once, myself included. It didn't feel strange that my self-worth was derived from other people's estimations of me. It felt very natural. My parents and I were happy—until the wheels came off. And suddenly, everyone became very unhappy.

The first time I experienced conditional love was when Daniel, my first boyfriend and first true love, handed me a note after third-period science class my freshman year in high school. We'd been dating for six months, and we regularly passed each other notes in between classes, but this note was different—so thick that it was popping open despite all the creative nips and tucks he'd put in place to hold it together. Inside, to my horror, he explained that while we'd "had some fun together," he didn't love me anymore, he'd become smitten with Shannon, a senior, and they were going to start dating. Anyone from the outside would say this situation, my first broken heart, was normal and even to be expected at this age, but it *did not* feel normal to me. It felt like a world of pain; it felt devastating.

Daniel might have told me he liked someone else more than me, but I read, in no uncertain terms, that I wasn't good enough and that I wasn't lovable.

A dragon was born inside me that day.

THE ROUGH ROAD AHEAD

Instead of turning the other cheek, getting over the breakup, and believing in myself more than some dude named Daniel did, my sensitive side kicked into overdrive, and I fed the dragon that was raging inside me by collecting stories, evidence, and experiences that I wasn't worthy of love—and never would be.

I didn't share my self-worth struggles with my parents for two reasons. First, the intensity of my heartbreak—how deep it cut, how bad it hurt—did not resemble my girlfriends' more typical reaction of feeling bad for a while but quickly moving on to their next relationship without much of a dent in their heart. By comparison, my pain seemed to affect me much, much worse, and at fifteen, I didn't know how to make sense of it. Second, I was terrified that my sadness would become my parents' sadness, and I refused to take that risk. We were the happy-go-lucky family everyone wanted to be around, and I was not going to be the daughter who disrupted that powerful and enviable force. So, I swallowed my suffering and did what I'd been doing for as long as I could remember—identifying an overly ambitious goal and hustling hard to achieve it, no matter the cost.

I decided then that I would find someone else to love me, and I set the bar really high. I believed that the greater the challenge, the better I would feel about myself when I accomplished my mission. I started looking for love in all the wrong places, most notably in the back seat of a Ford Bronco with *PLAYER* printed on the license plate. As you can imagine, that didn't work out for me in the long-term love department. Many other guys followed—each being more disrespectful, virtually untamable, and much older than the last. All this made my parents want to throw up.

Almost overnight, I went from a young girl with scores of accolades and accomplishments to a lying, sneaking, curfew-breaking, boyfriend-hopping teenager who disappointed my parents so deeply that they made it clear on several occasions that they didn't want to be around me. Looking back, it seems ironic that I was too scared to tell my parents that I felt broken on the inside, yet I proceeded to exhibit defiant and dangerous behavior that ultimately broke their trust and our relationship into a million little pieces. But, that's the way dragons work. They convince you that nobody wants to hear your busted-up sob story and that it's best to just shut your mouth, put your big girl pants on, and solve your damn problems yourself. This silent but desperate attempt to locate the love that was missing inside me did not make my problem of self-doubt go away. It made it worse.

I learned the hard way that if pride was what my parents valued most, then disappointment was their kryptonite. My worst nightmare had come true: my parents were exasperated and disappointed all the time, my big brother was off at college and no longer available for late-night bitch sessions, there was a shadow of darkness over my formerly happy home, and it was all my fault.

On the surface, my mom and dad could see that I was defiant, disobeyed their very reasonable rules, and lied regularly. However, what they couldn't see, and what I was unwilling to share with them, was that I felt so desperate to gain a sense of anyone's approval and affection that the consequences that stood in my way didn't threaten me. I was not afraid of being grounded. I was afraid of not being loved. Instead of revealing that a dragon of self-doubt had taken control of my life and my actions, I took the hits, I took the punishments, I took the judgment, and I never said anything. Being seen as defiant or a bad girl felt safer than being seen as someone who didn't love herself. For the people who raised me to be better and do better, the first was a phase and the latter was a burden.

Despite the darkness inside me, I still had lots of friends, regularly brought home straight A's, and continued to collect trophies like they were trading cards.

WAVING THE WHITE FLAG

Eventually, the dragon inside me grew bigger and braver until at age sixteen, it became all-consuming. My daily battle with my perceived inadequacies became too much to handle and overcome. I waved the white flag—not by asking for help, but by deciding to opt out. On a Tuesday night, I sat down at my white wicker desk in my pretty pink bedroom with matching floral curtains, dust ruffles, and pillow shams, and I penned five suicide letters. The list of recipients was short, as were the messages that held my final words. My parents; my brother; my best friend, Missy; and two previous boyfriends would all get similar swan songs summarized with the sentiment "It was a great life. I was loved. Please don't be sad. It was all just too hard for me." After tucking away the note cards in the drawer of my neatly organized desk, I walked downstairs in my floor-length white flannel nightgown, grabbed a green plastic cup from a cupboard in the kitchen, filled it with Sprite, and started swallowing pills from the pantry—three or four at a time. Advil? Check. Sinus medication? Check. My father's prescription heart medicine? Check. The more, the better. The quicker I could be gone, the faster I'd be free.

I've often heard people say that suicide is the most selfish thing one could do. As someone who invited death into her life before she really had a chance to live, I disagree. At sixteen, as I lay in a bedroom that would put Martha Stewart's best work to shame and prayed I wouldn't wake up, I believed I was doing my family a favor. I felt like a hindrance to their happiness and assumed life would be easier and better if I just went away. Trying to fight a dragon on my own wore me out. I was done. And I certainly was not afraid, because as someone once said, dying doesn't frighten those who are already half-dead.

I won't lie—I was pissed when I woke up the next morning. Absolutely pissed. I have no idea how my heart kept beating after being pummeled with a dangerous cocktail of pills. I never stopped to think about it—after my parents found my letters, they marched me right into therapy. I muscled my way through a few sessions, then quickly came up with plan B for dealing with this dragon. I had to figure out how to survive—specifically, how to keep my inner dragon off my back and everyone else happy at the same time. Since disappearing didn't work, I decided to show up with an even bigger, bolder "Look at me, I'm perfect!" persona.

Insert two decades of even more overachievement—extraordinary success both academically and professionally. I earned straight A's at the top graduate school in the country for my discipline and became the youngest vice president ever at the advertising agency where I worked on a team responsible for forty million dollars in revenue. My coping mechanisms for keeping my dragon at bay were simple: perform until there's no energy left to feel, make what is uncertain certain no matter the cost, and stay so busy that the truth of my hurting and fear of rejection can never catch up with me. Confiding in no one, not even my husband, I kept my struggles close to my chest and guarded them with my fake, facade-driven life. It was an exhausting but manageable existence. However, everything came to a screeching halt and my tactics ceased to be effective after giving birth to my first child and entering the most competitive sport around: motherhood.

NEWS FLASH: MOTHERHOOD AND SELF-DOUBT DON'T MIX

As a new mom, there was no time to shore up the energy necessary to maintain my facade. As a working mother, I moved at warp speed, juggling meetings, playdates, business trips, and family obligations. And at every frantic turn, I found myself dodging my dragon of self-doubt. It lurked behind my daughter's unwillingness to sleep in her own bed,

beneath my inability to get a healthy meal on the table, and in the lies
I told my peers about why I couldn't work late as often as I once did.
Clearly, the beast I thought I had pacified was simply lying in wait. I
found some validation from online "mommy blogs" and a handful of
celebrity parenting books, but the mom confessional trend was still in its
infancy at the time and mostly humor-driven.

I finally received the gift of perspective when I was asked by my
agency to conduct research with mothers from around the world in order
to help pitch and win the global Johnson & Johnson business. The agency
was looking to win a new account, but I was looking to save my soul. I saw
the assignment as an opportunity to pry into the minds of other moms
and learn how they managed to stay afloat in a way I no longer could.
I was exhausted from trying to prove myself at home and at work, and
the demands were taking their toll. Meanwhile, every mother around me
looked like Kelly Ripa on performance-enhancing drugs. I was tired, and
despite the love, affection, and support from my friends, family, and peers,
I felt very alone. This was an eerily familiar feeling, not unlike crying
myself to sleep as a teenager, then having to wake up the next day, pull
on my peppy cheerleading skirt, and get out there to make sure everyone
thought I was okay. Only this time, the person depending on me was a
needy infant who would die if I fell down on the job.

No pressure or anything.

I threw myself into the motherhood study and felt called to reinvent
traditional research along the way. Every expert marketer knows that
participants, especially mothers, lie in focus groups because they want to
look good in front of others. But I didn't want lies; I wanted answers. So
I asked moms from all over the world to share their highest highs and

lowest lows through an innovative form of qualitative research I developed called "Opinion Parties." During these parties, mom friends gather in the comfort of their own homes and dig deep to answer tough questions. The best part? Since the moms are already friends, they can skip the shyness, bypass the posturing, and get straight to the heart of dozens of topics.

Though I had selfishly hoped that my research would reveal the keys to a dragon-free kingdom, no such thing happened. Regardless of age, income, race, and nationality, all the mothers I studied were plagued with some sense of doubt. I heard "I feel like I'm a bad mother most of the time" from Berlin; "I wish I could stop beating myself up" from Paris; "I always feel like I should be doing more and that I can do better" from Korea. These mothers revealed their doubts and insecurities, and every last one confessed to putting up a facade and acting as if she had everything under control.

Within three hours of opening the research files, my office floor was covered with the deepest doubts I'd ever seen. There was nowhere to step, nowhere to walk, and nowhere to go—just me, down on my knees in a hurricane of pain. And I couldn't stop reading.

I worked late that night. I couldn't leave these women's bleeding hearts on my floor and return to life as I knew it. I'd seen too much, and I couldn't stop crying. I cried because I knew and felt their pain. Even moms who weren't plagued by a history of significant insecurity confessed to painting on a pretty face and acting as if they had everything under control. As a trained researcher, I didn't have to look hard to find the theme behind their stories. It was right on the surface: "We are not who we pretend to be." From Shanghai to Seattle, mothers everywhere were, in some sense, just like me.

After reading all I could take, I exhaled what felt like the very breath I'd been holding in since I was sixteen. It felt safe to come out of hiding. When I eventually turned off the lights at 2:00 a.m., I felt lighter than I had in years. As I left the office building, the security guard yelled from across the room, "My, my, Katherine, you're here awfully late. I hope you're okay." On any other day, I would have quipped, "Oh, yes, I'm fine! See you tomorrow!" But on this night, I decided to stop. I took a deep breath, looked her square in the eyes, and said, "I'm *okay*...but I'm very tired." The guard, a fellow mom, immediately stood up, walked around her desk, put her hands on my shoulders, and said, "I'm tired too. It sounds like we could both use a hug." And right then and there, she wrapped her strong arms around me, and we held each other up—in support of the long day we'd both had and all the long days that were ahead of us.

I felt embraced like I'd never been before, because a fellow mother, and fighter, was hugging the *real* me. This woman saw my truth, not my facade, and she appreciated and felt connected to what I showed her. In that moment, it was clear to me that she needed to hear what I had to say as much as I needed to say it. I might have been tired, but tired was so much better than alone.

In the end, our creative team brushed off the research insights in favor of sleek, glossy, high-design advertising that was ultimately shallow and lacking substance. We did not win the pitch, but that success metric was no longer important to me. I had uncovered the truth behind a growing population of modern mothers, and it had set me free. A creative director might not have known what to do with the insights I'd uncovered, but I knew exactly what to do with them. I would change the world with them.

LET THE SLAYING BEGIN!

The courage of those mothers in the research study was now a part of me, and I felt inspired to confront my own doubts, fears, and insecurities in a similar way. For the first time in my life, I was open to being honest about what plagued me on the inside. I was too tired to keep up the charade, and I knew that if I didn't find it in me to slay my beast of self-doubt—my dragon—once and for all, it would eat me alive.

The first catalyst for change happened a few weeks later. I had just spent two wonderful weeks with my family over Christmas break—away from the stress at work—and was hesitant to go back. I was in the kitchen making spaghetti when my husband, Richard, sensed I was down. When he asked what was wrong, I didn't hide and say "nothing" like I'd done the majority of our marriage. I answered honestly and said, "These past two weeks have been so great. I only had to focus on being a wife and a mother, and I really enjoyed it. But now I have to go back to work, and I'm worried I can't be a good wife, a good mom, and a good employee all at the same time."

His response was swift. "Just be yourself, Katherine. What is so wrong with being you?"

I didn't say anything aloud, but a very loud and clear voice inside said, *I don't like me.*

Those words shook me to the core, and I've since learned that their impact is known as a catalytic moment—a single point in time that changes your trajectory forever. And mine occurred only because I had the courage to admit I didn't like the situation I was in, which led to admitting I didn't like myself.

But given all I had and accomplished, *why?*

Instead of bolting from how I felt about myself, I ran straight to the self-help section of my local bookstore. And what I intended to be a quick trip turned into a two-year self-help journey that helped me slay the dragon that raged inside me. I dove into a massive stack of books about inner peace, compulsive behaviors, happiness, living in the present moment, living without armor, and living with self-compassion. I circled powerful passages, highlighted quotes that made me cry, and scribbled my answers to authors' questions on nearly every page. I stayed up late to read and woke up early to review. I crammed as much into my head and heart as I could because, frankly, I couldn't stop.

My second savior was Oprah. Each night, after putting the kids to bed, I tiptoed downstairs to watch reruns of *The Oprah Winfrey Show*. I must have binged on a hundred episodes over the course of six months. My routine was always the same—on the couch, under a blanket, red wine in my right hand and a box of tissues in my left. Each time Oprah asked an author, singer, heroic mother, or drug addict a question, I would silently answer the same question in my head. It's amazing how much you don't know about yourself until you've been interviewed by Oprah in your mind! I learned that I was desperate to impress other people because I was so unimpressed with myself; that I never learned how to deal with difficult emotions, only to avoid them; and that I wasn't so much addicted to titles and trophies as acceptance and approval. The more I learned, the more I developed courage to change—to rid my heart, soul, and mind of the crippling doubts controlling my life and my actions. I was still exhibiting the "Look at me, I'm perfect!" behaviors that I developed when I was sixteen, and I didn't want to feel like that girl anymore. I was a grown-ass woman, for God's sake.

My third savior was meditation, through which I felt the deepest and most powerful change. I'd collected enough shocking insights about my behavior to know that I wanted to be done with the dragon—the fear, anxiety, and denial, and living my life to please others. But being still and sitting in the silence took me to the next level. The answer to my most pressing question—*Why don't I like myself?*—came to me during a silent meditation session at a local community center.

I realized that all my pain, posturing, and perfectionism boiled down to the simple fact that when I stopped being me, I stopped liking me. I assumed that I needed to hide my broken parts to be loved, and I was *very good* at hiding. However, my investment in my brokenness and constant effort to disguise it kept my wholeness at a distance. In other words, I took the long, not-so-scenic, and rocky road to discovering a fundamental truth: you cannot love what you do not accept.

This had to end. As a wise woodsman once said, "If I had six hours to chop down a tree, I'd spend the first four hours sharpening the ax." I realized that I had just spent two years of nights and weekends uncovering my deepest, darkest secrets by working on myself in every way possible. I couldn't spend another minute harboring them. It was time to cut down some trees.

STANDING IN MY TRUTH

Six weeks later, I decided to take advantage of a speaking engagement for working mothers that I had previously booked under the headline "What Powerful Women Know That Others Don't." I scrapped my original speech and wrote a new one based on what I had learned from the Opinion Parties. It was a risky move—the event was intended to inspire and empower female employees to climb the corporate ladder with strategy and verve, and companies had paid handsomely to send their top executives to hear me, among others, speak.

As I stood onstage and revealed the truth about the dragons that lurk inside us, I could tell by the looks on the attendees' faces that my speech was not what they expected! But it was what they needed. I sensed a collective sigh of relief from the 250 women who sat before me, many of whom were mothers like you and me. I knew all too well how they felt because it was similar to what I had felt after reading the research results during the Johnson & Johnson project. The more I shared that day, the more the women relaxed; the deeper I went, the further they followed. When I made fun of failures, their faces said *I thought I was the only one.* When I admitted I was overwhelmed and exhausted, their eyes said *Me too.* And when I complained about companies always filling their commercials with picture-perfect mothers, their laughter said *Why the hell do they think that's what we want to see?*

My truth was their oxygen. I called on the women to share their own stories, and one by one, they supported each other, cheered one another on, and cried like beautiful babies. It was a roller coaster of an experience for all of us—unlike anything I'd ever seen. My own mother, whom I had invited as a special guest, went last. The woman who just witnessed her daughter share a chink in her armor for the first time wiped the tears from her eyes, stood up, and said, "I'm a mom, and I'm very proud of my daughter."

And there it was. *I had made her proud.*

On the surface, of course my mother would have been proud that I just delivered a big, well-received talk to over 250 women. However, what really happened on that stage was that, for the first time in my life, I shared my doubts, fears, insecurities, and broken bits—and it didn't scare, hurt, or break my mother like my dragon convinced me it would when I was sixteen. In that moment, when my mother accepted me warts and all, it dawned on me that she and my father had loved me all along. Of course, they disapproved and did not love the behavior I exhibited as a teenager, but they still loved *me*. There's a difference. I just couldn't see it at the time because a fire-breathing dragon was standing in my way.

Well, not anymore.

After the event was over, I sat in the parking lot, alone in my car, just sobbing and sobbing. For the first time in my career, I had given a speech for which my goal wasn't to shine, be admired, or win everyone's approval. My goal was to be honest and pay forward the gift of perspective that my research had given me. And in doing so, I had achieved the love, acceptance, and purpose I'd been longing for my whole life. It was a full-circle moment: I used the A-plus-seeking skills I'd honed as a child to work on myself in a way that made my mother and me proud, except this time, I did it for myself and other mothers. It reminded me of the brick in the sidewalk I so valued when I was ten years old, only this time, I didn't come this far to please others. I did it to be helpful, and my truth became my courage. I used my well-honed superpowers for good.

ONWARD AND UPWARD

I felt energized from the event, and I was convinced that I had to continue changing the world one mom at a time. After serving as an adjunct professor at the top advertising school in the country for nine years, I resigned. And after reaching the pinnacle of my career, I quit my job at the ad agency to become an entrepreneur. This was terrifying to a lot of people around me—my husband was scared about our financial security; my parents were worried what I would do for health insurance; and my friends were full of stories of small businesses going bust and mothers spending all their time with a start-up instead of their children. And while I had no idea how to run a company or ensure it would make money, I knew how to uncover rich insights about mothers, and I would figure out the rest as I went. I quit my job and became CEO of my dream come true.

I launched a company called The Mom Complex, where my team and I work alongside the largest product manufacturers and retailers in the world to turn the pain points of mothers into new products and services that make their lives easier. Our work has led to organic baby food that babies actually like, packable toys for busy families on the go, and shopping carts that safely hold an infant car seat without obstructing the view of the canned goods pyramid at the end of aisle twelve. Mothers get a better life, and companies get a better bottom line.

However, not every pain point can be solved with a new product, experience, or service. I've come to learn that mothers experience two types of pain points: external and internal. External pain points are the things others can solve for you, such as overly complicated dinner recipes and toys with too many small pieces that are easy to lose. Internal pain points are those you must solve yourself. These include the mean voice in your head that's constantly criticizing your every move, your lack of confidence in your decisions, and your inability to love yourself as unconditionally as you love your children. The Mom Complex will continue to take on the former. This book is designed to help you solve the latter.

ONE TEAM. ONE DREAM.

I've been a student of turning self-doubt into self-compassion for almost a decade now, studying and applying guidance from mindfulness, motherhood, spirituality, self-help, and meditation gurus. I regularly attend lectures, workshops, seminars, retreats, and conferences on these topics in order to stay up-to-date on the latest advice, words of wisdom, and helpful techniques. Even when I'm designing and facilitating my own workshops and I'm technically the teacher, I'm still a student— learning about the inner workings of women's minds and finding the most efficient and effective paths to freedom.

As part of my work toward eradicating the internal pain points of mothers, I want to help you live your very best life. I believe we end up teaching others the very thing we most need to learn. I love teaching mothers how to slay their self-doubt and increase their self-compassion because it's a lesson I missed out on for so much of my life. And to this day, I still need and benefit from constant reminders. Once I stopped living to impress others and started embracing and owning my own truths, doubts, and insecurities, a remarkable full-circle experience opened up. The initial research helped me. I helped myself. Now, I want to help you.

For entirely too many years, I waited for a boyfriend in high school, a straight-A report card in college, or a senior vice president title at work to shield me from a fire-breathing dragon of self-doubt. But, as it turns out, I didn't need a knight in shining armor to save me. I just needed a sword so I could save myself. And that's all you need too.

BE THE *slayer* YOU WANT TO SEE IN THE WORLD.

CHAPTER 2

Meet Your Dragon

For more than a decade, I've been studying the lives of well-meaning mothers who self-sabotage their happiness, yet one of my biggest *aha* moments occurred when I climbed aboard a whale-watching boat in Mexico a few years ago. On a beautiful, sun-kissed morning, my husband and I were greeted by a smart, charming, and passionate guide named Lisa. I believe you can tell a lot about a person from the first thirty seconds of an encounter, but I needed less than half that time to discern that Lisa was put on this earth to teach people about the fascinating behaviors and habits of whales. A marine biologist who traveled the world to document whale migration and educate others, Lisa confessed that it was her life's work to share what she has learned for one very simple reason. "I believe that what you know, you love," she said. "And what you love, you protect."

I nearly fell off the boat.

Lisa instantly went from whale-watching guide to spiritual guru— she might as well have been talking about dragons. Suddenly, everything I had studied and battled reached a new level of understanding. As mothers, we often don't understand ourselves well enough to know what we should be loving and protecting beyond our children and families. In its simplest form, my own path to freedom from self-doubt boiled down to (1) knowing myself, (2) loving myself, and (3) protecting myself—in that order, just like Lisa said. The problem is that too many of us have been skipping the first step.

Up until that point, most self-help experts I had met and read about insisted that the need to love yourself was paramount to a meaningful and graceful human existence, and I agreed. But you can't even go there until you know who you are and what makes you tick. It's funny because, as a mother, you know what pizza toppings your son hates, exactly what your daughter is thinking when she slams her bedroom door, and the price of their favorite granola bars at four different grocery stores. Yet most of us have far less insight into the historical nuances of our self-doubt—where it came from, when it first appeared, when it escalated, and how it reached its peak. It's clear from my research that the primary reason you suffer was likely active in your life long before you had kids, but, as a mother, you now have hundreds of new, pressure-packed situations to feel insecure about. So where did it all begin? Before you set out to love the mother and woman that you are, let's find out what gave birth to the dragon that gobbled up your gusto in the first place.

WHERE DO DRAGONS COME FROM?

Nearly every mom who attends my workshops can quickly identify the series of events that sent her self-esteem on a downward spiral. For some, it stemmed from traumatic events—parents who fought their way through a dramatic divorce; bullying; physical, emotional, or sexual abuse; and the list goes on. For others, smaller insults packed a powerful punch—snide laughs, snarky glances, and words that were said or unsaid by those whose opinions they valued. In fact, your self-doubt might have begun with something so seemingly slight that even speaking of it makes you feel ashamed because relative to, say, bullying and abuse, it feels rather insignificant.

Based on my own experience and that of thousands of mothers I've interviewed, dragons are often born when a difficult situation collides with a deeply sensitive soul. Meaning, a difficult experience in your life, one that would challenge anyone, took you down in a different way—it cut deeper, lasted longer, and hurt more. You may remember this first incident because it marked a line in the sand. Before your dragon was born, life didn't seem to feel so stressful, dramatic, or painful. But after that initial bout of self-doubt, your dragon managed to take over and insist that you'd never feel whole, worthy, or filled with long-lasting satisfaction again. It could have happened as a child, teenager, young woman, or new mother. The possibilities are endless for how your fear started holding you and your happiness back, but pinpointing the beginning is the key to putting it to an end.

Both nature and nurture set the stage for self-doubt. If you have the tendency to turn your struggles into suffering and you find yourself surrounded by angst, worry, and constant fear that you're going to screw something up, then you were either born this way or made to feel this way—or a little of both. The good news is that these scenarios are mostly penetrable, and with the right tools and support, you can leverage what happened to begin a better, easier, and more fulfilling life.

In this chapter, I'll help you revisit pivotal points that gave birth to your dragon. But don't worry: we won't stay there long, because no matter how much time you spend unlocking the pain of your past, you must keep an eye on your future, because that's where your healing resides. At the end of the day, while it might not be your fault that you were born or raised to behave a certain way, it is your choice to stay that way.

HOW'D YOU GET SO SENSITIVE?

As I mentioned earlier, there's a 20 percent chance that, in the words of Lady Gaga, "Baby, you were born this way." According to acclaimed journalist and author Anneli Rufus, one in five people are born with a propensity toward doubt, insecurity, and low self-esteem—just as some are more likely to sing like a lark or go bald. These "highly sensitive" individuals possess a genetic trait that causes their brain to regulate serotonin and dopamine in a way that contributes to their nervous system picking up more subtleties in the world. In other words, your brain is wired to take in the highest highs and lowest lows and reflect on them more deeply. And when you *really* feel the emotional roller coaster of your life, it increases your propensity for shame, fear, perfectionism, doubt, and other self-esteem crushers.

Even if you're not a card-carrying member of the hypersensitivity club, it's highly likely that you're more sensitive than many of the men in your life. Decades of scientific and biological research show that women's brains are wired differently from those of our male counterparts, making us more prone to doubt, worry, and irrational fear.

According to MRI-based research conducted at the University of California, Irvine, in 2005 by psychology professor Richard Haier, men's brains use seven times more gray matter than women's. This is the part of the brain that processes information locally, in specific sections. It explains why men tend to be better at focusing on one specific task, can't multitask as well as women, and, when feeling emotional, may choose to change course and do something active rather than analyze their feelings. (I'm sure you have no idea what I'm talking about here.) On the other hand, women's brains use ten times more white matter.

This is the networking grid that connects processing centers across different parts of the brain. The result? The female brain is more likely to stew and get stuck on emotional memories.

So, there you have it—a perfectly feasible explanation for why your husband shuts down and goes to the gym after a fight while you mentally replay the entire conversation and potential demise of your marriage until he returns. The way I like to explain these biological differences to my workshop attendees is this: your brother's, husband's, and father's brains have more one-way streets through them, while yours has a lot more intersections and thus a lot more traffic jams. As a result, we get emotionally backed up. Life's trials and tribulations stir us, rock us, and constantly cause us to question whether we're making the right choice. I'm not a therapist, but I can't help wondering if this is related to the fact that teenage girls are far more likely to suffer from depression. According to a 2017 study on sex differences and depression published by the journal *Translational Psychiatry*, 13 percent of boys and a staggering 36 percent of girls have been or are depressed by the time they hit age seventeen.

Whether you're genetically predisposed to being supersensitive or have reason to believe you are, it's very likely that this characteristic has been frowned on over the years—perhaps it's been seen as a weakness or a trait that holds you back in life. Maybe your big brother called you a sissy when he saw you cry after a flower died, or maybe your parents told you to grin and bear it when you sulked in your bedroom after feeling left out at a school dance. Or maybe your boss told you to keep your emotions in check or avoid taking things too personally while giving advice on what it takes to get ahead. This kind of thinking by far too many people we know, love, and respect—not to mention societies as a whole—sends a clear message that being sensitive is bad.

Honestly? I call bullshit on all of it. Those comments, likely delivered by people missing their own sensitivity chips, occurred in your past, and it's time to look to the future. And when you do, make no mistake—being a sensitive human being is not a problem. It's a gift, a blessing that allows you to soak up all that life has to offer, see deeply into situations and other people, and demonstrate empathy toward your loved ones and even total strangers. Not surprisingly, it also makes you a better mother.

This nature probably also means that you cry a lot—or at least I do (just ask my husband). I cry at happy events, such as watching my daughter go pee-pee on the potty for the first time; hard times, such as finding the courage to quit my job; heroic moments, such as watching strangers cross the finish line at a marathon; manipulative triggers, such as sappy television commercials; and don't even get me started when it comes to death. I used to apologize for being a weeping willow, but now that my dragon of self-doubt doesn't tell me I'm a loser because of it, I no longer hide it. I finally know myself well enough to know that if I didn't cry so much, it would mean that I was asleep at the wheel.

BRACING FOR IMPACT

Regardless of how or why you developed your sensitive soul, it was likely shocked to its core when it collided with a difficult situation related to family members, friends, or peers. Maybe you stumbled over your words while reading out loud in fourth grade, everyone laughed, and you've felt academically insecure ever since. Perhaps a group of mean girls called you fat in middle school and you never looked at yourself with loving eyes again. It's also possible that your first love dumped you via a Dear John letter after gym class (*ahem*, I'm looking at you, Daniel) and you spent years looking for love in all the wrong places.

It could also be that your initial and very deep blow was more direct and came from the very people who made or raised you. I've heard horror stories from mothers whose parents regularly referred to them as the stupid one, bad one, dumb one, or selfish one in their family. It doesn't take a psychologist to tell you that labels like that stick, hurt, and can cause intense psychological damage that could last a lifetime. Even nonverbal cues that give off feelings of disappointment leave painful and indelible scars. Your parents might have expressed love and affection when you stayed within the confines of their expectations, but if you veered off course by doing something wrong—from spilling cereal on the floor to getting arrested—they may have resorted to slamming cabinet doors or rolling their eyes until they fell back into their heads.

And, even if you were blessed enough to escape childhood insults because you were surrounded by loving family, supportive teachers, and nice friends, your self-doubting ways could have developed as a young woman when comparing yourself to others left you feeling like a loser. How many times have you stood in the checkout line at the grocery store in your sweatpants and headband, glaring at the women on magazine covers who surely smelled like rose petals on their worst day, or watching a mother on the playground discipline her son in a calm, cool, and collected tone as you realize your own son has only ever heard you yell when you're setting him straight.

The mom role itself can be a trigger too. Sienna, a mother of three who came to one of my workshops, never recalled feeling inadequate as a kid and felt loved as an adult. It took a surprise pregnancy to dramatically alter her self-image. "Being a mom changed everything. I was suddenly lost, life felt impossible, and I felt wholly inadequate," she said. "I went from being a confident woman to an exhausted single mom, while all my other friends my age were getting married and buying their first homes. I let my life get off track, and I started to resent myself for it, even though I loved my son and wouldn't have traded him for the world. It was a very overwhelming time."

Sienna eventually found the courage to slay her dragon by accepting and seeing her single status as an asset instead of a deficit. She threw herself into new experiences—photography, yoga, and belly dancing classes—which boosted her confidence, momentarily freed her of her mom identity, and introduced her to a wider swath of friends. Feeding her own happiness gave her the space to enjoy the time she spent parenting.

So, here's what I want to know: Who stole *your* joy? What could have knowingly, or unknowingly, stripped you of your self-confidence, self-esteem, and the light inside your soul? Nobody is watching you or reading this. Write it down here:

. . . .

. . . .

. . . .

It's okay to acknowledge it. Don't feel bad about it for one second.

Pinpointing the individual or event that stomped all over your self-esteem is critical for understanding what that experience taught you and why you feel the need to hide it from the world. In my case, experiencing back-to-back blows from my boyfriend and then my parents broke me in half, and the shrapnel it sprayed fueled my irrational fear that rejection and loss were lurking around every corner. What fear are you trying to desperately tuck away, cover up, and hide from the rest of the world?

THE EVIDENCE YOUR DRAGON LEAVES BEHIND

Regardless of how long ago your dragon was born, it's important to understand how it's affecting your life in the here and now. As I mentioned before, dragons and the suffering they cause can show up in different ways for different mothers. Sometimes, there's a clear-cut, direct correlation between how your dragon came to be and how it shows up. For example, if your mother made you paranoid about men loving and leaving you, your marriage may suffer; if your father screamed at you all the time, you may feel like a horrible human being when you raise your voice at your daughter; and if someone called you fat, you might be terrified of entering the dating pool after divorce. And sometimes, there's no obvious correlation. So, if you got cut from the gymnastics team as a teenager, you might still be trying to make up for it by landing the top sales position at work. Dragons are tricky like that.

Regardless of how it came to be, what is consistent with every dragon-battling mother I've ever interviewed is that something stole her self-esteem, and by exhibiting fierce determination and setting expectations that are entirely too high, she's working around the clock to try to get it back. All the extra effort exerted, most of it unnecessary, is a desperate attempt to show anyone who will pay attention—her children, partner, mother, brother, her son's preschool teacher, or the cashier at Trader Joe's—that she does indeed deserve to be seen, loved, and appreciated.

I've created the following checklist that will help you determine the extent to which doubt, insecurity, and fear play a starring role in how you view yourself as a mom—which, of course, continues to seep into other roles in your life. See how many apply to you.

HOW TO SPOT A DRAGON CHECKLIST

Check all that apply:

☐ You're a people pleaser by day and an overthinker by night.

☐ Your mouth says yay even when your gut says nay.

☐ The negative voice in your head is the meanest mean girl you know.

☐ What other people think of you carries more weight than what you think of you.

☐ You're behind on your to-do list before your feet hit the ground in the morning.

☐ The longest you've ever been proud of one of your accomplishments is six minutes.

☐ You point out everything you do wrong and nothing you do right.

☐ One day, everyone will realize you're not as smart or pretty or nice as they think you are.

☐ You're tired. Like fall-down-after-running-a-marathon tired.

☐ You feel broken and believe you must hide that brokenness to be loved.

So, how did you do? If two or more of the above accurately represent how you're approaching, dealing with, or defending against the life in front of you, it's a really good thing you picked up this book! Know, too, that while some of these traits feel natural, they are not healthy. Your life doesn't have to be *this* hard, I promise.

CHANGE IS IN THE AIR

Now that you've identified how your dragon was born and how it's showing up in your life, it's time to move beyond what happened in the past and start making changes for the future. How will you know when you're ready to start slaying? When you're sick and tired of being afraid, when you're tired of working your ass off all day, every day, and *still* feeling like you should be doing more, and when moving forward might feel scary but staying where you are feels impossible.

I often refer to mothers who suffer from self-doubt as the "walking wounded" because at one point in their lives, someone hurt them, they never addressed the wound, and therefore it never healed. And unfortunately, as I know all too well, when you deny pain in your life, everything you do or think becomes influenced by it. For years, I did whatever it took to hide my wounds, but trust me when I tell you that wounds can be healed. And when they are, you will begin to experience life in a whole new way. When you're no longer contaminated by the idea that you need to please, prove, and perfect your way through life, you begin to see small, magical moments of joy in everyday occasions. Recently, I've found them at the end of an exercise class when I quietly thank myself for taking the time to work out, when I walk down the street and listen to the birds instead of the messages on my phone, and when my son says that I'm the best mother in the world and nothing inside me, not even the tiniest whisper, begs to differ. Now *that* is winning.

Comedian, actor, and talk show host Chelsea Handler is a woman who many might assume, given all that she's accomplished, is free from nagging thoughts of self-doubt. Yet she has opened up on Instagram to prove otherwise. In a rare sign of gorgeous vulnerability from a woman of such influence, she made it clear to millions that while she might flirt with self-doubt, she refuses to let it control her life, decisions, or day. She posted:

> *Some days I really don't feel like getting out of bed. Some days I don't think I'm doing enough. Some days I feel like I don't know enough. Some days I feel like I'm not strong enough. Some days I feel like I'm not pretty enough. I'm not smart enough, I'm not thin enough, I'm not doing enough. And on those days, I get my ass out of bed, look myself in the mirror, and remind myself that's not the person I want to be. I want to be a badass. I define me. You define you.*

We need more honesty and bravery like this in the world, from moms and non-moms alike. Watching any other woman conquer her dragons gives the rest of us the courage to believe we can do the same.

HOW TO MEASURE SUCCESS

If you had a choice, would you choose joy or suffering, ease or unease, peace or conflict? The truth is you do have a choice. You always have—and as I mentioned before, all the tools you need are inside you. Trying to slay your dragon with external solutions when the problem is internal will never work. Turning to things outside yourself for relief such as more impressive titles at work, deeper massages at the spa, and bigger bottles of red wine will not save you; these things will only distract you. You cannot turn your attention elsewhere in pursuit of inner peace because it is within your own body, mind, and soul.

When it's time to jump into part 2 of the book, which will help you identify the ways you're feeding your hungry dragon and how to stop, you'll likely wonder how to measure your success. If you're like a lot of the mothers I work with, keeping track of how you feel will motivate you to keep going and growing every step of the way. The only measure of your success should be the degree of peace you feel within. For twenty years, I lived with a ferocious, manipulative, lying, and dangerous creature that stole my joy and pushed me to work entirely too hard to prove I was worthy of other people's love, only to realize later that peace of mind was all I ever really sought. Learning to assess my inner state of peace is by far my greatest accomplishment, and I have nothing outwardly to show for it—just soft, quiet, and spectacular inner peace deep inside.

Not a bad way to start each day.

BEING SENSITIVE ISN'T A PROBLEM.

It's a gift.

CHAPTER 3

The Fine Line between Struggling and Suffering

*W*hen it comes to being a mother, the struggle is real. It's a nonstop, never-knowing, always-anticipating, and completely exhausting operation. It's been hard since moms protected their kids from storms by sleeping in caves, and it will continue to be hard when moms are nursing their newborns in the back seats of flying cars. You go, girls! What's less obvious, and rarely if ever discussed, is something I've seen play out in my research studies for years: the difference between struggling and suffering. There's a distinct and often dangerous difference at play, and if you want to quiet the steady drumbeat of dread in your mind, then you can't confuse the two. Struggling is to be expected. Suffering, however, is self-perpetuated, and it makes your job harder than it has to be. All moms find their kids' actions confusing, challenging, and at times annoying—meaning they struggle. But they don't all turn their frustrations into a personal indictment and proof that they flat-out suck. That is suffering, and it's time to make it stop.

There's a fine line between struggling and suffering, and one of my goals is to make sure you make it a *firm* line that you cross as infrequently as possible. That way, you can protect, defend, and honor the beautiful soul that's inside you and tired of getting beaten up every day. To succeed at this involves recognizing your behavior when it happens so that you can mitigate it.

What you don't want, but I suspect you feel, is for suffering to be the main theme of your story as a mother and person. You don't want to suffer more than you struggle, because the more time you spend suffering, the more time you'll spend battling your dragon with your happiness hanging in the balance. And as we've established, ain't nobody got time for that.

STRUGGLING VERSUS SUFFERING— WHAT'S THE DIFFERENCE?

I like to follow a simple rule for distinguishing between struggling and suffering that shows there's more than alliterative semantics at play here. Struggles represent the chaos *around* you—the challenges that your eyes can see, such as the toddler who won't get in his car seat or a teen's bad report card. Suffering, on the other hand, represents the chaos *inside* you. It's the pain your soul feels when you don't believe you're smart enough, tough enough, or patient enough to deal with the struggles that come with the grueling job of being a mother.

For instance, grocery shopping with two tired and hungry kids under the age of four and leaving the store without threatening to set their toys on fire is a struggle. Every mom, no matter how put together she felt when she left the house, will rightfully fall apart in this scenario and need to come up with an action plan to wrangle the external forces working against her. However, silently screaming insults *at yourself* when you can't get the kids to calm down in this circumstance is an exercise in suffering. Browbeating yourself into thinking another mother would do a better job is suffering. And allowing this self-flagellation to make you feel so lousy that you have a hard time believing your kids or spouse when they compliment or say they love you—yup, more suffering. The thing is, suffering is needless, self-inflicted, and incredibly painful. You know you're picking at yourself like a crusty old scab, and yet you can't seem to stop. Sound familiar? Let's see if you recognize yourself in any of these situations:

Struggling: "I have nothing for dinner as usual. Looks like chicken nuggets and frozen broccoli again—maybe this time they'll eat it with hummus. Here goes nothing…"
Suffering: "I'm a poor excuse for a mother because my friend Kelsey's kids devour broccoli like it's candy, while mine yell at me for even putting it on their plate."

Struggling: "If my mom says one more thing about my son's grades, I'm going to start buying wine in bulk."
Suffering: "I've really let my son's standards slip—even my own mother sees it. We both know he'll probably end up in jail by the time he's sixteen, and it will all be my fault."

Struggling: "Can my boss stop emailing me 24/7? He needs to cool it. He knows I'm at the doctor."
Suffering: "I know the gyno has her hand on my boob right now, but I need to email my boss back ASAP because everyone else at work is at the top of their email game, and it's a miracle I still have a job."

As you can see, your response to the challenge in front of you is what defines whether you struggle or suffer—and whether you destroy or feed your dragon.

Lauren, a working mother of two who attended one of my workshops, was brave enough to share the tightrope she was walking between struggling and suffering in hopes of healing from the battle she was waging with herself. As Lauren explained it, she was recently out of town on a business trip when her husband and nanny both managed to screw up the explicit instructions she left for her daughter's kindergarten spirit week. Lauren held nothing back as she shared her story. "I did everything for them!" she shouted. "I laid out each and every outfit right next to the list with the themes for each day. Meanwhile, on Monday, superhero day, I get a picture of my daughter wearing the clothes for Friday, which was red, white, and blue day. My daughter missed superhero day and the associated yearbook photo because my nanny sent her in the wrong clothes. I know it doesn't matter what the teachers, room mothers, and principal thought when my child was the only one not dressed up—literally…the only one. Yet, I found myself lying in my hotel room, staring at the ceiling and berating myself for not being there for my kids, convincing myself I was a terrible mother, and questioning when in the hell I was going to get my act together. It felt like it was my fault, despite the fact that two grown-ups were left in charge of the plan. Why does it take two people to do my job when I'm gone and it *still* gets botched?"

I asked Lauren to join me at the front of the room and face me, hold my hands, and shut her eyes. As she obliged, I saw a kind yet skeptical look come over her face. Next, I slowly and lovingly breathed life into her shame-filled soul by telling her the truth. I explained that there is a fine line between struggling and suffering, and she'd gone to the other side. Struggling says "This shit is hard." Suffering says "I'm doing a shitty job." Struggling is working your ass off to get ahead of the game, laying out every outfit before you leave town, leaving specific instructions, and finding out that mistakes still happened. Suffering is berating and blaming yourself for not doing, planning, or being enough…or having the belief that you could have done, said, or planned more. As I told Lauren, "You were a good mom that day, the following day, and every day since. You did everything you could. You should be proud of that, and you did it on top of winning new business for your company. You did enough. You are enough. Now, stop beating yourself up for not doing more."

Tears streamed down Lauren's face, and the room was silent long after I finished. Lauren realized that she'd sabotaged her own joy and happiness and that by not admitting it was hard, she'd made it harder. I asked the other mothers what they learned from Lauren's story. One raised her hand and shared, "Silence is the conduit that turns struggling into suffering." She's right. Your silence will not protect you; it will only hurt you and the people you love. When you talk about your struggles, it reduces their power over you. Think of these admissions as a test run. If you can't admit the visible pain points that every mother struggles with, you will have a much harder time admitting what's lurking beneath those struggles. You have to start somewhere.

THE STRUGGLE IS REAL

It's okay to admit that being a mother is a struggle, because it *is* a struggle. And you are not alone, even if you think this 937 times a day. In fact, not only is motherhood hard, but it's also harder than it has been in years past. According to the Bureau of Labor Statistics, mothers today are spending more time at work—75 percent of mothers were in the workforce in 2016 compared to 19 percent in 1950. Meanwhile, according to *The Economist*, we're spending twice as much time with our children as we did in 1965. Wow! And spending more time with your children—preparing multiple meals, driving to extracurricular activities, supervising homework, and leaving work to attend Valentine's Day parties at school—is not a U.S. phenomenon. Spikes have been documented in Canada, the UK, Denmark, Norway, France, Germany, the Netherlands, Italy, and Spain. These shifting tides are in line with an "intensive parenting" ideology in which today's parents dedicate an increased amount of time with their children because they believe it's critical for positive cognitive, behavioral, and academic outcomes.

I don't know about you, but I cannot recall one single moment when my parents nervously hovered over the kitchen table as I completed my math facts homework, yet I find myself doing it all the time with my own kids, paranoid they'll fall behind. And don't even get me started about how long it takes each week to organize my family's calendar to make sure everyone's in the right place at the right time across their sixty-two weekly activities. Sound familiar? This intense parenting trend leaves very little time for you to breathe, brush teeth, or, heaven forbid, do something nice for yourself such as buy a new orchid to replace the one you killed.

In addition to being time-starved, we're often solution-starved when confronted with pressure-packed parenting dilemmas, the likes of which our own parents rarely had (or if they did, they seemed to process and internalize them differently than we do). An increased presence and awareness of upsetting scenarios such as bullying and school shoot-ings, learning difficulties such as ADD and ADHD, and deadly peanut, dairy, and gluten allergies leave us without a playbook, with nowhere to turn, and with more questions than answers. The number of these cases is skyrocketing—according to the Centers for Disease Control and Prevention, there was a 50 percent increase in childhood allergies from 1997 to 2011, and in 2013, 3.5 million children were on medica-tion for attention deficit disorders compared to 600,000 in 1990—and it's leading to a decision fatigue I see all the time in otherwise smart, sane, and confident mothers. No matter how calculating and rational you try to be, you cannot make so many new decisions without paying a physical and emotional price.

And if these practical pain points aren't enough to wear you down, according to a 2015 study conducted by Edison Research, 68 percent of mothers on social media feel their parenting decisions are being judged by other mothers online. They end up wondering whether they're breast-feeding too long or not long enough, if the school lunches they pack are worthy of a Facebook post, and whether their new jeans look too much like mom jeans. These are questions we ask ourselves every day, and they can throw any well-meaning, well-dressed mom off course.

So if motherhood feels like a struggle as you work in the home, out of the home, and around the clock to deal with a multitude of decisions—according to the *Wall Street Journal*, that number is thirty-five thousand decisions a day—you're simply a bona fide member of the motherhood club. Welcome to the fact that struggling is most mothers' normal, and regardless of age, race, income, nationality, geography, and marital status, we're all subjected to it.

TOUGH DAY IN THE LIFE

At The Mom Complex, we've conducted extensive research into a mother's day by way of a research app that moms carry around in their pockets and purses for ten days to input their most pressing highs and lows. The chart below represents the average frequency and intensity of passion versus pain that's felt in any given twenty-four hours, regardless of whether the moms were rich or poor, bottle-feeding or breastfeeding, urban or suburban, married or divorced, working outside or inside the home.

PASSION

7:00 A.M.   11:00 P.M.

PAIN

Do you see what I see? That's right: there's more pain than passion in our lives. It turns out that teaching tiny humans how to function in the world is hard, and you cannot buy, trade, beg, borrow, or steal your way out of the struggle that comes along with doing hard things.

In fact, the top five pain points or struggles in a mother's day boil down to this:

1. **Dinnertime.** All the buying, plotting, planning, burning, arguing, fussing, fighting, and forgiving that goes with often being the only one who cares about getting food on the table.

2. **Fighting.** All the guilt that comes with yelling at your partner, raising your voice at your daughter, losing your mind with your son, and watching your children clobber each other.

3. **Forgetfulness.** All the extra work that comes with realizing you bought peanut butter but not jelly, forgetting to sign a permission slip, and blanking on your sister's birthday because your mind is so jam-packed.

4. **Calendar-izing.** All the mind-numbing time it takes to get requests from kids, partners, grandparents, teachers, friends, community events, letters, emails, and texts onto the family calendar so everyone knows what to do and where to go.

5. **School Communication.** All the frustration, worry, and angst that's created when communication from your child's school comes home in bits and scraps of paper shoved in the bottom of backpacks, and you're supposed to keep track of every last one and not miss a beat.

This information is not meant to overwhelm you (although it makes me tired just writing it); in fact, it's intended to inspire you! I know moms, and if there's one thing I've learned from studying them with the passion that Jane Goodall studies apes, it's that you're not weird, inept, or a loser because you're struggling. In fact, learning to handle the struggles without dipping into suffering is the ultimate goal. In the challenging arena of raising happy and healthy human beings, including yourself, that's what winning looks like. We'll dive into how to stay in the struggle zone in later chapters, but for now, I suggest that you repeat this mantra when you need a reminder that the external chaos in your life isn't about you: Motherhood is hard—not because you're doing it wrong, but because it's just plain hard.

SLIPPING INTO SUFFERING

Now, the question becomes whether you're making motherhood harder than it has to be. You? Could that be? Stay with me here, because I may be about to shock those slippers right off your feet. I've come to learn that suffering comes and goes for all mothers and often flows in a circular pattern. As you can see in the chart below, it's very easy for your struggling to roll into suffering—and then for the energy behind that suffering to feed more struggles that cause you to suffer even more.

STRUGGLING
(EXTERNAL FORCES)

SUFFERING
(INTERNAL FORCES)

But there's also the line that exists between the two categories, and the minute you cross over it, you're face to face with your dragon—a gnarly, sneaky beast who hangs out below the surface amid your darkest feelings. It's where your doubt, fear, and shame like to hide.

What makes one mom suffer isn't necessarily the same for another—many of us feed our dragons in different ways, as we'll explore in part 2 of the book. One mom might beat herself up when she loses her temper with her son because her own mother did the same with her, so it triggers a past trauma and self-rebuke because she desperately wants to do better. Another mom might suffer in the kitchen because her mother-in-law is a real gourmet, which makes her worry that she's not living up to her role as the family matriarch in a way that her husband is accustomed to. Unfortunately, the opportunities are endless.

However, no struggle has to drop down into suffering unless you let it. That's right, you get to decide whether dinnertime sucks or you suck for not making it look like a highly styled scene out of a cheesy television commercial. Among mothers who regularly cross the divide from struggling into suffering, an unmistakable characteristic they share is their ability to quickly notice where they fall short but almost never where they succeed.

I'll never forget the first time I ran a workshop with two hundred moms and asked them to scribble the answer to this fill-in-the-blank sentence on a Post-it Note. It read *I'm not _____ enough.* The exercise took thirty minutes longer than I expected because attendees kept raising their hands, not to share, but to ask for more Post-its! There were enough on each table to sink a battleship, yet those women kept wanting more time and more paper, because their laundry list of inadequacies was *that* long. Eventually, the women bared their souls to a room full of mostly strangers and explained that they didn't feel nice enough, tough enough, rich enough, thin enough, successful enough, supportive enough, around enough, whole enough, pretty enough, wife enough, sister enough, daughter enough, or mother enough. These were women who suffered, not struggled. There were a lot of tears that night, so I tried to end the session on a high note.

I scanned the room and called on a woman named Leslie since she was the sole mother out of two hundred with only one Post-it in her hand. Surely she would demonstrate to all the other mothers how to self-contain one's pain. Talk about a miscalculation! Leslie stood up, sheepishly looked down at her orange slip of paper, and said, "The only thing I could think to do was cross out the blank space in the middle. So, my Post-it Note says 'I'm not enough.'" Conversation immediately erupted in the room as the other 199 moms attempted to lift Leslie's spirits by telling her she was great at her job, cooked a mean meat loaf, and looked stunning in her pantsuit. However, their sympathetic ways lasted approximately thirty-five seconds before the commentary turned from "Poor Leslie" to "Way to go, Leslie! Why didn't I think of that?" It was hard to watch but easy to understand—it hurts our hearts to hear others say they're not good enough, but as mothers, we have *no problem* repeating that same damaging rhetoric to ourselves. The answer on a Post-it Note that made the other women want to help Leslie because it was *that* bad also disappointed them because they hadn't thought of it for themselves because it was *that* good.

TIME TO LOOK IN THE MIRROR

World-renowned author and motivational coach Tony Robbins says that our lives are defined by the stories we tell ourselves. Words matter, and if you tell yourself that you're incompetent at your job, you're not going to ask for a raise. If you believe you look horrible in everything you put on, you're not going to step into the dating pool. If you don't think you're smart enough, you'll stay late at work trying to prove that you are. And if you think you're a lousy mother, you'll dismiss your best friend's compliment about handling the PTA meeting with style and grace. The actions you take are motivated by images in your mind. And guess who puts those images there? You and only you.

Which brings me to this: I need to take a minute to throw down a little truth here. While suffering rears its ugly head within some of the hardest working and well-meaning mothers I know, their suffering doesn't have as much to do with their desire to be better for their family as they tell themselves. You are at the center of your suffering, and the way you feel about you doesn't do *anyone* around you any good. In other words, suffering doesn't make you a better mother. I'm willing to bet that your home isn't more efficiently run, your children's rooms are not any cleaner, and your partner doesn't help out more because of how bad you feel about yourself and the pressure that comes with that. What *will* help you do better for your family is seeing and trusting the bright light, the goodness, that's already inside you so you can put your best foot forward and give you, your family, and your life the very best you have to offer. When you can accept that the suffering is put there by you, that's precisely the catalyst you need to begin making the life-changing shift away from fear and toward freedom.

The day you realize you're the source of your suffering is the first day of your healing. Frankly, saying you're not the cause of your suffering sounds a lot like your four-year-old saying she had nothing to do with the two rolls of toilet paper that found their way into your toilet. Remember how I shared in the last chapter that the minute I realized

I'd stopped being me is when I stopped liking me? It's not a coincidence that the word *I* appears twice in that single sentence. I was the culprit, and I had to realize it before I could become the catalyst for change. It will take work to get there, but this was an eye-opening revelation for me, and I've seen it carry the same power with women all around the world.

While it might feel overwhelming to know you're the source of your suffering, it should also feel liberating. If you cause it, then you can own it and *un*cause it. You're in command of every thought, action, and behavior that fills your life. When you do the work to understand and eradicate your suffering, you'll see that life is lighter, brighter, easier, and more beautiful without the blinders of self-doubt on. To drive this message home, I'd like to introduce an exercise I regularly use during my workshops. The goal is to look at the factors that are hard in your life and identify how you might be making them harder than they have to be—meaning, when you're crossing the line from struggling to suffering. I inserted Lauren's example that we discussed earlier in this chapter. Take a minute to complete the rest using recent examples from your life.

STEP 1: WHAT'S HARD
IN YOUR LIFE RIGHT NOW?

Example: Kindergarten spirit week

1. ....

   ....

2. ....

   ....

STEP 2: HOW ARE YOU MAKING THOSE CHALLENGES HARDER THAN THEY HAVE TO BE?

Example: Feeling like I failed my daughter because I wasn't home to get her dressed.

1. ....

....

2. ....

....

STEP THREE: HOW CAN YOU MAKE THESE SITUATIONS EASIER?

Example: Ask for help. Invite my partner or babysitter to help prepare the outfits so it's not all on me and they can get more familiar.

1. ....

....

2. ....

....

Now that you've mapped out your suffering, see if you notice any themes or hints related to what your suffering stems from. For Lauren, her deep desire to feel worthy was causing her to tightly control the outcomes of every struggle in her life. But yours could be completely different. Your answers above contain clues, and the clues are important for two reasons. First, the way you relate to your struggles *is* the issue, meaning it will define your reaction, response, and self-worth.

Second, if left unaddressed, you'll end up repeating the same suffering theme in various areas of your life—not just parenting—until you're willing to stop. So, what's your theme?

The theme behind my suffering is:

....

....

....

....

What's important here is taking responsibility for your own suffering. Think about the struggles in your life—whether it's spirit weeks, fund-raisers, out-of-town soccer tournaments, or a boss who is missing a sensitivity chip—and you'll realize that they all come into your reality as neutral. Now, if given a blank canvas and asked to paint the details and facts of these scenes onto it, what colors would you use? Black for fear, red for anger, blue for disappointment, yellow for optimism, or perhaps silver to indicate that you'd do your best to find the silver lining within the struggle? Never forget that you're in charge, and you're the painter. You're the Monet or even Bob Ross of your life! The universe hands you blank canvases all the time, so pay attention to what colors you're using to tell your story—the brighter and more vibrant, the better.

OUR SUFFERING ADDS UP

If your struggles represent the chaos around you and your suffering represents the chaos within you, then it's important to understand that there's a cumulative effect when the two combine and $1 + 1 = 15$ on the scale of pain you're causing in your life. Spirit weeks are a struggle, but when you pile your doubts, fears, and insecurities on top of the buying, organizing, plotting, and planning that's required, the task in front of you grows so big and ugly that it feels insurmountable. It makes your "motherload" that much heavier—it's like putting on a backpack with a ten-pound weight inside and carrying it while you complete the 156 things you need to accomplish. You think you're tired because you have a lot going on, but really, you're tired because you're working overtime fending off a fire-breathing dragon while you're signing permission slips, attending parent-teacher conferences, organizing sleepovers, and cleaning up the shaving cream in your bathroom from your daughter's slime-making science experiment.

The next time you find yourself suffering, pause to evaluate what's going on beneath the surface. Is your suffering causing more struggling? Here's a quick scenario for you to try on for size. Let's say you walk into your house after a long day of work and either (1) you're proud of the job you did at the office today, and you're tired but happy with your performance after a long day's work or (2) you're behind on a project and a palpable fear of failure is coursing through your veins and turning your stomach into knots. During dinner, your daughter makes it clear that she doesn't like the pork chops you made and she prefers the ones that Bailey's mom makes. *Ouch.* How you react to this depends on what's going on inside you. If you're confident in who you are and believe you made the best meal you could, then you're more likely to have the strength to say, "Sarah, be quiet and eat your dinner." However, if there's a dragon of self-doubt raging inside you on a mission to collect evidence, stories, and proof that you're a poor excuse for a human being, then you're more likely to turn into a fiery ball of rage and scorch the earth around your daughter's dining room chair and threaten her life if she ever says such a thing again.

Not that I've ever been there or anything.

We think we can hide the dragon, but we can't. My dragon used to make regular appearances at the dinner table when, after a long day of feeling less-than-enough at work, my children said they didn't like what I had prepared. Let's just say my exasperated and over-the-top defensive response wasn't pretty. The punishment of my harsh words and condescending stares did not fit the crime because I had redefined the crime. My children said they didn't like asparagus, but I heard that I was a poor excuse for a mother. I wasn't happy with myself in general, and their distaste for the meal was just another proof point that I was falling down on the job. Unable to understand why I was so mean during dinnertime, my husband finally suggested, "Honey, maybe we'd all be happier if we let the babysitter feed the kids before we get home." Conflict on the inside creates conflict on the outside.

I'm happy to report, however, that the opposite is also true: when there is calm on the inside, there will be calm on the outside. Therefore, when the battle is won within, it will cease to exist in the rest of your life. In his 2013 book *Within: A Spiritual Awakening to Love & Weight Loss*, noted integrative doctor Dr. Habib Sadeghi explains that "the involution always precedes the evolution"—meaning, if you get your thoughts and intentions in line with who you want to be, the rest will follow suit. Amen to that. I have just as many struggles in my life as I had when I was living with my dragon of self-doubt—my children still don't particularly care for vegetables, the laundry piles up more than I'd like, field trip forms jammed into the bottom of a backpack continue to make me bonkers, and I still have to hire, fire, evaluate, and train people at work. However, by having the courage to understand, recognize, and minimize the invisible parts of my life (my suffering), the visible parts of my life (my struggling) all got a lot easier. There's simply less friction turning up the heat and making them harder. Soon, this will be your truth too.

Now that you know where your dragon came from and how it's dragging you down, it's time to put this beast of yours to rest. In part 2 of the book, you'll discover seven ways you're feeding your dragon and how to stop. Are you ready to do this? Knowledge is power, and the more you understand what's keeping your dragon around, the sooner you can make it go away.

THE STRUGGLE IS *real.*

YOUR SUFFERING IS *optional.*

PART II

SEVEN WAYS YOU'RE

Feeding Your Dragon

AND HOW TO

Stop

CHAPTER 4

You Set Superhero Expectations in a Mortal's World

*P*lenty of women set high expectations for themselves, and this can be a tremendous asset. It helps motivate you to breastfeed twins, eat brussels sprouts to set an example for your kids, and pull your little ones away from the TV even though it makes completing your chores a nightmare. And make no mistake, these are all good things.

It's when you create *unrealistic goals* for yourself that you drop into a tailspin of trying, falling short, and trying all over again while whispering to yourself, "See, I told you that you suck." If you're already operating from a deficit of self-doubt, setting expectations you're incapable of achieving will do little more than give your dragon the ammunition it needs to continue kicking your ass.

I speak from entirely too much experience when I tell you that setting ridiculous expectations will always get in the way of you being your happiest self. For two long decades, I suffered at the hands of sky-high expectations that even Wonder Woman couldn't come close to conquering. After years of advice from my real therapist as well as my imaginary one (Oprah), I'm now capable of admitting that the suffering I'd been feeling as a mom was self-inflicted. I repeatedly set the bar too high, I fell short on the regular, and I called myself a loser for not measuring up. And while I knew it was on me to either deliver or drop the ball, it took outside intervention and a lot of self-reflection to realize it was *also* on me to stop setting my expectations so high. Playing the blame game gets you nowhere. Nobody can make you do anything. Even if someone has a gun to your head in a dark alley, you still get to decide whether to give them your wallet or take the bullet.

The only keepsakes my ridiculous expectations left behind were impossibly long to-do lists that ended up in the trash. Oh wait, they also left me with bone-tired fatigue, bags under my eyes, a constant unsettled feeling that I could and should do more, and more gray hair than any of my friends. Vanity aside, and more than anything, never living up to my own impossible standards made most days feel like a big, fat burden. And that's just no way to go about your day.

As far as I'm concerned, the mythical expectation that mothers need to have all the answers is both dated and destructive. I can't stand the phrase "Mom knows best" because it puts even more pressure on you to work harder at being perfect. Trying to figure out impossible answers only invites suffering. And frankly, even after trying, I'm not sure we *do* know what's best. At least not for ourselves. But that can change. I used to give a standing ovation in my living room when Oprah would have Maya Angelou, world-renowned activist and author, on her show. Without fail, Maya would always share her life-changing *When you know better, you do better* mantra with the audience. Remember that as you read this book. Your journey toward inner peace should begin in your head and end with your feet.

As we set out to tackle the seven major ways you're feeding your dragon and how to stop, know that there's a reason why adjusting your crazy expectations is the first stone to overturn. Expectations are everything—and by everything, I mean the root of all evil and suffering.

Why? Because the filter through which you see yourself as a woman and mom is based on how you feel you *should be* performing in these demanding roles. If you're living with a dragon of self-doubt, then your expectations are distorted and not based in reality. They're based in anticipation and anchored by hurt. Think of your expectations as a film or residue that coats the floor-length mirror in your bedroom. The more frequently you let yourself down for not achieving your lofty goals, the thicker it gets and the more disappointed you feel about the person you see reflected back. But with all that gunk in the way, how can you see the real you?

In this chapter, you're going to wipe away the grime that's obscuring your most beautiful and true self by setting more realistic expectations. Notice that I didn't say *lowering your expectations*—or, God forbid, *settling*. We all know that ordering a pizza every night and phoning in a subpar performance on your next presentation at work won't benefit anyone. Raising happy, healthy, and kind children who can make their own breakfast is important work, and you want to do it well. With expectations in check, you'll continue to accomplish great things and have the sense of satisfaction that comes from being ambitious; you'll simply drop the pretense and expectation that being perfect or being seen as perfect will make you happy.

By setting more realistic expectations and achieving them, you'll finally, for once in your exhaustive existence, be able to recognize and love yourself for who you really are. And the best part? Aligning your expectations with reality will not only help you put your daily decisions in the win column, but also gain the strength and courage you need to beat down your dragon for good.

THE PERFECT MOM PARADOX

If you've ever thought that you were the only one fighting sky-high expectations as a mom, think again. I've studied mothers in seventeen countries including India, Korea, France, Italy, Brazil, and Switzerland—in other words, all over the damn place—and millions of them suffer from what I call the Perfect Mom Paradox.

Here's how it works: When you first become a mother, your expectations are ridiculously high. You're going to make your own baby food, establish a solid sleep schedule from day one, and losing all that baby weight? Not a problem. It's going to melt away like butter on hot toast when you take advantage of the free childcare at your gym four days a week.

No one can fault you for this line of thinking because it's only natural that you'd want to do motherhood well. Frankly, it would be strange if you didn't. The problem is that when you're a new mom, the "baby brain" you're fighting that makes you put your phone in the fridge and pour orange juice on your cereal is also causing you to forget that you've never raised a child before. In other words, you're setting your expectations sky-high for a job you've never auditioned for, attempted, or spent one day doing before now. P.S. Babysitting and owning a dog do *not* count.

To be clear, all moms suffer from the Perfect Mom Paradox, not just moms fighting dragons. It's perfectly normal, universal, and sane. The chart on the next page illustrates this phenomenon—one that few moms talk about yet everyone I meet experiences. As you'll see, the initial gap between expectations and experience is where the paradox, and the suffering, coexist.

If misery loves company, take heart that you're in really good company among other new moms who beat themselves up over high expectations. And if you've read anything by world-renowned spiritual guru and *New York Times* bestselling author Eckhart Tolle, you'll recognize that the Perfect Mom Paradox isn't so far off from Tolle's definition of—wait for it—*human suffering.* Tolle says that when you long for a life that is different from and better than the one you're currently living, it creates friction and angst inside you. Makes sense, right? And yet new mothers choose to live and breathe the very definition of human suffering every day.

There's a popular quote pinned on mothers' Pinterest boards around the world that says *Sleep won't help if it's your soul that's tired.* Truer words have never been posted. Personally, I'm a fantastic sleeper, always have been—I'm talking eight to ten hours straight without even getting up to pee. However, before I defeated my dragon, I spent half my life suffering from a bone-tired fatigue that would make most grown men faint. Make no mistake about the truth I'm about to drop: the Perfect Mom Paradox is the reason your soul is so tired. Stop saying it's because you spend so much time running errands, drudging over meals in the kitchen, or the illogical but oppressive dread of slightly annoying tasks such as replying to your mother-in-law's email.

The physical demands of motherhood are taxing, but they don't tire your soul. It's the warped belief that you can and should be doing better that keeps you down.

For new moms, there comes a day when all this changes. You're able to wear an outfit that isn't made of spandex, plop your child in a shopping cart, and complete your grocery shopping without bursting into tears. This is when you've moved to the right side of the chart— meaning, your experience is greater than your expectations. When you're living on this side of the paradox, it feels like relief, like winning the sack race at your fifth-grade field day. Or putting on a new pair of jeans and knowing you look good in them. And yes, sometimes better than sex.

The truth is, the Perfect Mom Paradox will continue to ebb and flow throughout your life. It resurfaces each time you're forced to deal with a situation you've never faced before. I'd bet that your heart is intimately familiar with these highs and lows, but it takes a while for your brain to process and accept this. Here's what it looks like for the visual learners in the crowd.

BABIES   GRADE SCHOOLERS   TEENS   ADULT CHILDREN

All moms are first-time moms at some point because we're constantly dealing with firsts—even when we have multiple kids and think we've been there before. In truth, experience earns you little reassurance because you're immediately onto the next unknown. Once you think you've managed toddler meltdowns at preschool, you're on to navigating the teachers, room mothers, homework, field days, mystery reader sign-up sheets, and spirit days of kindergarten (I mean, *why?*), all while your other child deals with the death of her first pet or refuses to hold your hand in public, which breaks your heart. Even once your kids are grown, they'll lean on you when times are tough—if they're suffering from infertility, were turned down for a promotion, or are going through a divorce. Once a mom, always a mom—and apparently, always a new mom too. According to my research, one of the first realistic expectations you should set for yourself is that you're never going to have motherhood all figured out because you're always going to be a rookie. And rookies don't get things right the first time.

HOW HIGH IS TOO HIGH?

Just like there's a line between struggling and suffering, there's a subtle but substantial difference between expectations that are high and ones that are too high. As you might guess, those who suffer with dragons swing into the too high category, and not just during firsts or in certain vulnerable circumstances like discipline or academics. They do this almost across the board and as a matter of course.

Remember, it's okay to work hard to achieve your goals—I want you to have high standards and be your best self too. What I don't want is for you to work around the clock to fail at the unachievable. The first step to adjusting expectations is being able to identify the difference between high and too high. Below are examples from my workshops.

High: "I'll go back to school to get my master's degree while raising two kids."

Too High: "I'll get straight A's while getting my master's and never miss a school activity or sports event."

High: "I'll leave my job to stay home with the kids without losing my mind."

Too High: "Having me at home will make everything better. The house will always be clean, homework always done, pickups on time, and a healthy dinner on the table."

High: "I am going to hold down the fort financially while my hubby looks for a new job."

Too High: "I'm going to nail every assignment at work so I can get a raise to help pay the bills while also covering all the laundry, dishes, dinner, and duties at home."

High: "When the alarm goes off at 6:00 a.m., I'll squeeze in as many errands as I can."

Too High: "I've got a hundred things to do today, and napping is for losers."

It's a fine line and fascinating difference that's not about semantics. When your expectations are too high, you live in the suffering zone and you prevent yourself from reaching the point in parenting when you realize that the job is insanely hard for everyone. You never say it's okay to have a messy home or feel beaten down by your daily duties. You never tell yourself you're doing your best and that your best is good enough because you don't feel you're good enough. And you certainly don't ask for help from the friends, family, and other moms around you, because help is for moms who need it, and you don't. Just like I didn't.

The question you need to answer for yourself is why. Why can't you ask for help from your friends, family, partner, or other mothers? Probably because you're terrified of other people thinking you don't know what you're doing. But here's motherhood's dirty little secret: nobody knows what they're doing, because they've never done it before. Period—end of story. As mothers, we've got to stop trying to be know-it-alls when we don't know it all.

SO WHAT ARE YOUR EXPECTATIONS?

The best way I know to confront your expectations is to get clear on them and commit to better ones in writing. I'm not afraid to get naked in front of you, so I'll go first. Several years ago, when my life coach asked me to quickly jot down my expectations for motherhood and myself in general, here's what I scribbled down on printer paper in my home office:

> **My expectations for motherhood:** Joyful, rewarding, fulfilling, easy. I've never heard anyone—my mother, grandmother, other mothers—say it's hard, so I think it's probably supposed to be pretty easy.

My expectations for myself: Be a good mother every hour of every day in everyone's eyes.

Looking back, those statements still send a slight pain through my heart. What a heavy load I was carrying, in addition to being a mother of two young kids and with an intense career. Now, I'd like for you to try this exercise. Be honest. Moving from darkness to light is a brave move to make.

My expectations for motherhood:

....

....

....

....

My expectations for myself:

....

....

....

....

How does it feel to see your expectations in writing like this? Kind of crazy, right? One clear sign that your expectations are not aligned with reality is when you use absolute language to describe them, such as *best*, *most*, *always*, or *never*, or when you drop external approval cues, such as *everyone*, *my kids*, *my husband*, or *my mother*. Nobody is perfect, and nothing can be done well all the time. Your self-satisfaction depends on accepting and believing this.

I'm sure you noticed the link between the two statements above. If you believe motherhood as a job should be easy, breezy, and beautiful, then your expectations as a mother will be higher. The equation seems clear enough: if it's *supposed* to be easy, you *should be* very good at it, right? Wrong. There are no absolutes in parenting, and it's hard as hell. One key to letting yourself off the perfection hook is to admit that the job itself is insanely challenging.

SKY-HIGH EXPECTATIONS IN ACTION

When a participant in one of my dragon-slaying workshops shared her story of self-inflicted suffering, it was clear to me that she struggled with sky-high expectations that affected both her sense of self and her family. Elizabeth shared that while she was sitting in a late-afternoon meeting at work one day, her phone rang, buzzed, and beeped until she finally answered it. It was the athletic director at her son's new school, telling Elizabeth that she forgot to pick him up from basketball practice. She gasped, grabbed her purse, and flew out the door as though her life depended on it, because as she later realized, her self-worth actually did depend on it. During her nine-mile drive to the school, Elizabeth gave herself a real tongue-lashing: *What the hell is wrong with you? How could you forget about your child? What are the other moms going to think? You're a horrible mother.*

Elizabeth was embarrassed to reveal her mistake to her husband, Doug, when he got home that night, but she quickly was glad she did. Upon hearing the news, he simply shrugged his shoulders. "People make mistakes," he said. "We just moved to this city two months ago. The school is new to us, the routine is new to us, having three kids in school at the same time is new to us, and the schedule changed at the last minute. Give yourself some grace."

As Elizabeth shared her story, the other moms breathed a sigh of relief. Based on the theory of the Perfect Mom Paradox, they surmised that while Elizabeth had been a mother for seven years, she had only been a mother to a second grader in a new city for a whopping five days. Given that newfound context, Doug's suggestion—*give yourself some grace*—felt like a gift from above and was one that they said they'd start applying to their lives that very night.

Giving yourself grace when challenges show up in your life—first-time or otherwise—helps naturally adjust your expectations of nailing them on the first try. Suffering exists not because you're experiencing something hard but because you refuse to admit that you are experiencing it at all. There's a difference.

So here's your opportunity for a full-frontal confessional: What obstacles are you experiencing right now in your life? Any area is fair game—home, work, marriage, friends, kids, passions of yours. You're a human *and* a mother, which means you have more firsts than just the maternal ones.

1. ....

2. ....

3. ....

4. ....

This is the first step in stopping the madness behind saying that you *should know* how to handle challenges in your life. To quote Carrie

Bradshaw from *Sex and the City*, we as women must stop "*should*ing all over ourselves." This is even more pertinent for moms.

A LITTLE PERSPECTIVE CAN'T HURT

Rejiggering the longtime expectations you've had for yourself will not come easy and will often feel the opposite of natural. One thing I suggest when you're getting started is to gain some perspective from the people around you. In my case, I started with a loved one who lacked significant life experience but came to the table with strong opinions—my five-year-old daughter.

One evening, while I was feeling bad about myself for not keeping a spotless home, preparing dinner from scratch every night, and reading chapter books during bedtime, I found myself in my daughter's bed begging for compliments. "What makes me a good mom?" I asked. Was I leading the witness? You bet, but I needed to feel better about myself. My daughter's response was swift and to the point. "You're nice to me, and you buy me pink clothes," she said without missing a beat. Holy crap. My daughter's expectation for my performance as a mother was to deploy kind words on cue and buy her a tacky T-shirt every once in a while.

Try this technique. No matter what your child's age (brace yourself for snarky answers with teens), I think you'll find that they don't care if you rearranged their stuffed animals after they sloppily made their beds or if you serve them fresh organic green beans over the frozen ones. In fact, on that last one, I'm pretty sure they'd prefer if you dropped the ball entirely. Your children want you to love them, and if they had any idea what goes on between your ears every day, they'd start begging you to love yourself more too.

DON'T BE YOUR OWN WRECKING BALL

You've been telling yourself for years that your extreme expectations are in place for the well-being of your children or your family. But that's not the full story. We've talked already about where your dragon of self-doubt came from, and perhaps that's who you're trying to prove yourself to these days. For example, if your mother made you feel like you weren't good enough as a little girl, you might now think that when she sees your homemade pomegranate Popsicles and impeccably decorated Christmas tree, she'll *finally* realize how wrong she always was!

Yet according to my research, it's far more likely that you're overreaching to impress yourself and not the demons from your past (see also *past bullies, ex-husband, ninth-grade boyfriend…*). You're convinced that if you can do the impossible, then perhaps you're better at this mom gig—and ultimately, at life—than you originally thought. Did your past feed this? Of course. But you're a grown-up now, which means you're accountable to no one but yourself. So now you're attempting to complete Herculean efforts to win *yourself* over. When you experienced the difficult situation that gave birth to your dragon, it cut you so deeply that you lost confidence in yourself, and every day since, you've been clamoring, clawing, and ratcheting up your expectations with all your might to exceed them so you can finally feel better.

The only problem is that your efforts to set yourself up for success are setting you up for failure. Believe it or not, this is empowering news. If you're the one setting the bar so high, and you're the one you're trying to impress, then you're the only person who can bring your expectations back down to earth and find joy, happiness, and an extra spring in your step when you do.

MORE REALISTIC EXPECTATIONS

It's time to set expectations that will make you feel good about them while also starving your dragon, who wants nothing more than to feed on your despair. Remember when I shared my motherhood and personal expectations earlier in the chapter and asked you to do the same? Here's what I came up with after working with my life coach to set new, more achievable expectations based on reality, not on trying to prove myself anymore:

My expectations for motherhood: *I expect that it's going to be a shit show. I expect that I'm always going to need help, and I'm always going to ask for it.*

Expectations for myself: *I expect to do the best I can. I expect that I'm going to lose my patience and temper from time to time. I expect that every day is going to bring a challenge that I won't know how to deal with. I expect that I will not be perfect, and I'm okay with that.*

Now it's your turn. What expectations will provide relief instead of suffering? How can you set the bar so that you can clear it and land on that nasty dragon, squishing it in the process?

My expectations for motherhood:

....

....

....

....

My expectations for myself:

....

....

....

....

WHEN WINNING STILL FEELS LIKE LOSING

Even with your new expectations in writing, you might still be saying, "I get it, but what's *really* so wrong with aiming for the stars?" It's a valid question. The answer is simple, yet somehow just as confusing as why Starbucks forces you to say "I'll take a tall" when ordering a small coffee. The problem with super-high expectations is that sometimes you succeed and actually achieve them. Every once in a while, when you lose enough sleep, practice more than you should, and hurt yourself enough…you win. You become the senior vice president you always wanted to be; you make it to the regional tennis tournament like you said you would; you receive your sought-after standing ovation for leading the fund-raising efforts at your son's school. And let me just tell you what you already know: it's like crack. I've never smoked crack before, but I think it's exactly the same. You feel like a rock star, high on life, proving to everyone who previously discounted you that you're a frigging diva. The next Beyoncé in the making.

But, the high quickly disappears.

You remain super proud of yourself for approximately eight days, nine at the most, and then start asking yourself *What's next?* because you're playing a zero-sum game in which your losses far outweigh your wins. Meaning, you want, long for, and *n-e-e-d* the next win to feel worthy. You're only as good as your most recent win, and apparently, that was eight days ago…so get on with it. What are you waiting for?

When you need that next win in order to feel worthy, you set your expectations too high in every area of your life—from parenting to relationships and beyond. There is so much you're good at, but you're only focusing on where you fall short. In doing so, you ignore that your expertise as a mother comes in waves; you wear yourself out trying to do and be more; you continue to fall short and berate yourself for doing so. And…the cycle continues.

GET ACTIONABLE

Here are some tools to help you adjust your expectations. They were, and continue to be, invaluable to the happiness I missed out on for so long. I hope they're helpful for you too.

* **Put your expectations in writing.** Before embarking on a new adventure such as a new job or joining a gym, write down what you expect from yourself and what you'll get out of the experience. If your expectations stay in your head, they'll be too high. By writing them in your journal, on an index card, or even a gum wrapper, you can keep them grounded. It will also help you commit to them in the same way making a to-do list keeps your tasks top of mind. For example, in this very moment, I'm in the middle of writing my first book and I have a Post-it Note on my computer that says *I expect this to be hard*. Because writing

seventy-five thousand words isn't easy, and I don't want to lose sight of that. Literally.

* **Expect things to go wrong.** When my children reached the age when they were arguing all the time, regular evening fights were new and frustrating to me. So when entering the house after a long day at work, with my hand on the doorknob, I'd take a deep breath and silently say to myself, *I expect things are going to get messy tonight.* It worked like a charm, because eighteen minutes later, when my children were screaming and yelling at each other over the rights to a busted-up stuffed teddy bear, instead of beating myself up for raising animals for children, I simply said, "Yep, I knew this was coming."

* **Expect to ask for help.** Accepting that motherhood is unpredictable, full of foibles, and too big for one woman to tackle is critical to finding and nurturing self-compassion. Kate, a mother of three who attended one of my workshops, once explained that waiting in traffic and carpool lines while picking up her son from soccer at 6:30 p.m. stressed her out beyond belief. So she switched things up, asking the babysitter to pick up her son while she went straight home from work to be with the other kids and start dinner.

THE ULTIMATE LITMUS TEST

Once you're done with this book and out in the world regularly setting new expectations, you might ask yourself the very logical question *When I'm faced with new situations and need to set new expectations, how will I know if they're so high that I'll inevitably feel let down by chasing them?* My advice is to deploy this litmus test that works every time. Simply ask yourself *What's my intention here? Why am I doing this in the first place?* Did you sign up to be the room mother at your son's school because you want to spend more time with him or because you want to make sure all the other moms see that you're a good mom? Are you forcing your daughter to eat spinach every night because you want her to have strong bones and a healthy immune system or because it's what good mothers are supposed to do?

When the intentions behind your expectations come from your truest self—the part of you that knows you're capable of being a great mom and are already a great mom—your expectations will be in line with what's best for you and your family because they'll come from the most pure, honest, and genuine part of you, not the part that's got something to prove. On the other hand, if your intentions stem from your self-conscious self—the part that wants to make up for something in the past or look good in front of other people—your expectations skyrocket because they're based in fear and are an attempt to make up for your inadequacies.

Adjusting your expectations with the right intentions forces you to make yourself a priority. How about that? You'll breathe more deeply than ever, finally and fully seeing your own greatness. You'll appreciate what you're doing well and put the less-than-well scenarios in perspective. Those experiences will no longer stick to you like glue and infect every-thing you touch like they did in the past.

Feeling satisfied and sane at the end of the day is worth so much more than going to bed with a perfectly vacuumed kitchen or having baked a birthday cake from scratch. And speaking of finding more sanity in your life, when your expectations are aligned with reality, your dragon will have a whole lot less to bitch about. Which is where we're going next.

IT'S NOT
empowering
TO THINK
YOU CAN
ALWAYS DO
MORE. IT'S
ACTUALLY
exhausting.

CHAPTER 5

You Quietly Yell at Yourself—All Day, Every Day

*I*t's time to talk about the voice in your head.

Everyone has one, so there's no point denying it. If you think you're somehow immune to this phenomenon, then the voice in your head probably just made itself known and sneered, *Oh, whatever. I don't have a voice in my head. Only crazy people have voices in their heads.* We all have a soundtrack of thoughts, feelings, and emotions that pop up throughout the day, providing colorful commentary on everything from the cleanliness of your car, to your husband's haircut, to your daughter's obsession with mascara. Sometimes it's helpful, and other times it's negative. And when your dragon has its way, it's downright destructive.

According to mindfulness gurus and psychologists alike, your inner voice might be called your *inner dialogue, the voices within, mind chatter,* or, my personal favorite, *monkey mind,* according to Buddha himself, who, 2,500 years ago, described the human mind as being filled with drunken monkeys—jumping around, screeching, and chattering on endlessly. (Oh, you know me so well, Buddha.) Regardless of what you call it, the voice in your head takes on different forms throughout the day. Sometimes the narration you hear can be neutral and purely observational, as in *Look! Those are the silver shoes I wanted to buy.* Occasionally, it can be positive and downright complimentary like *Damn, I pulled together a stellar silver outfit to wear with my new shoes.* However, the vast majority of the time, our inner voice-overs have nothing but negative things to say, such as *Who in the hell wears all silver to a wedding? You look like a female version of the Tin Man, and you dance like one too.*

Perhaps you'll find it comforting to know that you're not alone in your ability to annihilate yourself. According to the National Science Foundation, the average person has between twenty thousand and sixty thousand thoughts per day—and 80 percent of those are negative! A fact that instantly explains, and somewhat excuses, the thoughts you had yesterday about your son's stubbornness, your sister's wardrobe, and why people go fishing. However, be very careful about letting this fool you into thinking it's not necessary or possible to teach the voice in your head some manners. I'm living proof that it can be done, as are the thousands of mothers I've helped along the way.

It's been my experience that moms who battle dragons not only have negative inner voices that are louder than most, but they also succumb to their advice and criticism more often than they should. If you're longing for a life with less friction and more inner peace, aim to reduce the negative voice in your mind so you can begin to hear and rely on the more positive voice that's struggling to break through —your intuition. We'll explore dialing up your intuition in part 3 of the book, but for now, it's enough to know that there is a kinder voice inside you just waiting to guide, console, and reassure your way toward your best self. We just need to get your mind to shut up so your soul can have a chance to speak.

In this chapter, you'll see that when it comes to curbing negative self-talk, awareness is more than half the battle, and you'll be pleased at how simple it is to make big changes in a short time. Once you understand when your negative voice is most likely to rear its ugly head, you can encourage it to chill out. Of course, none of this will alter the amount of crap you need to accomplish in a day, but you'll begin to achieve those tasks with far more ease, grace, and gratitude—and fewer tears, moans, and groans.

WHY SO NEGATIVE, MAMA?

While the constant negativity might weigh you and your self-esteem down, believe it or not, it happens for a very positive reason. What if I told you it's a biological imperative? And that the reason everyone with a pulse feels tempted to hold on to the negativity is that our brains are wired to stick to negative experiences like Velcro, while repelling the positive ones like Teflon.

According to Rick Hanson, PhD, *New York Times* bestselling author and founder of the Wellspring Institute for Neuroscience and Contemplative Wisdom, all humans are evolutionarily wired with what's termed a negativity bias—meaning, your mind is naturally designed to focus on the bad, discard the good, and prepare for the worst. Hanson explains that it's a built-in survival technique that dates back to when our ancestors had to rely on instinctual judgment to stay alive. While preparing for the worst might have helped those long ago avoid flash floods and cougar attacks, mothers today tell me their nagging voices serve little purpose other than to burden their health, happiness, and sanity.

It's likely you've had a negative voice in your head for as long as you can remember. Various psychological studies find that mental chatter begins around age two or three and has the ability to turn negative at age five when children reach a sense of self-esteem comparable in strength to adults. This is the age at which you start seeing yourself in relationship to others and start judging yourself. Need a quick trip down memory lane? How about the tongue-lashing you got when your best friend developed boobs before you? The back talk you silently served up when you didn't get into your first college of choice? The *maybe I'll be single forever* thoughts when your boyfriend was taking his sweet time before proposing? Whether these negative reactions were fueled by a natural survival technique or by your deepest doubts and fears, the point is that smack-talking yourself is nothing new. But, that's no excuse to let it continue.

There's no time like the present to put an end to your self-sabotaging behaviors, because if you're anything like the mothers who attend my workshops, motherhood has taken your smack talk to an entirely different stratosphere. Being a mother is a constant juggle, and it's perfectly natural and even healthy for you to question and occasionally critique how well you're keeping those balls in the air. However, telling yourself that you're unfit for the job, an embarrassment, or screwing everything up while you simultaneously parade around like you have everything under control is unhealthy.

So here's my question. If millions of mothers are falling victim to dragon induced, fear-based thoughts, then why does this behavior remain one of the deepest and darkest secrets lurking inside some of the hardest-working and well-meaning people on the planet? What's holding mothers back from outing our dragons' sneak attacks and getting the help and encouragement we need to call a cease-fire?

Maybe you're embarrassed, maybe you think you should know better, or maybe you're convinced you'll put a stop to all the bad-mouthing tomorrow, just like you're going to start that new diet on Tuesday. However, according to my research, it's more likely that you're simply unaware of how negative the rhetoric has become and the damage it's doing to your self-esteem. You're too busy washing, brushing, cooking, cleaning, mending, dragging, dropping, and running to notice. It's become an unconscious behavior, and it's hard to change what you don't acknowledge.

CRITICAL VERSUS CRUEL

While we all have an instinctual negativity bias, if you have a dragon of self-doubt, the voice in your head goes from critical to cruel in a nanosecond. In other words, you bypass the thought *I've got to get better about remembering the dates for my son's field trips* and jump directly to *You forgot again? How can you be so disorganized? Other mothers find the time to remember.* It's time to start recognizing and dissecting the difference between these two examples of mind chatter.

Reminding yourself to do better next time can be helpful; however, attacking your soul for what you perceive as unrelenting failure becomes deeply ingrained in your psyche and yet another reason you think you suck. The dragon-fighting women who attend my workshops go so far as using the words *cruel, condescending, hurtful, vicious, ugly, relentless,* and *bullying* to describe what they secretly and regularly say to themselves. The voices in their heads bypass critical and take a nosedive into cruelty because they're being influenced by past failures, perceived inadequacies, and a deeply entrenched belief that they're not good enough and never will be.

Having a critical voice in your head can feel annoying, tiring, and less than awesome. But it is manageable and at times beneficial. However, having a fire-breathing dragon that intentionally puts on painful soundtracks set to the rhythm of *Why can't you get your act together, lady?* is a different experience altogether. It leaves you exasperated, exhausted, and constantly ratcheting your expectations higher so you can eventually prove it wrong and finally get it to shut the heck up.

Just know that your dragon loves and even encourages mean and manipulative self-talk, because telling yourself that you're stupid, ugly, fat, or unworthy of love chips away at your happiness, confidence, and energy. Your dragon *needs* you to feel badly about yourself so it can stay alive. So long as you're too weak to slay it, it can continue to control your life and your sanity. If you have a cruel voice in your head, it comes from your dragon playing DJ on what I like to refer to as your "bitch radio." And, as important as it is to change the station, it's hard because it's become such a familiar part of who you are, and even frenemics offer their own kind of safety.

As you embark on this journey, keep in mind that you're never going to get rid of the negativity altogether (remember, it's there to help you survive), so moving forward, your goal will be to keep the volume and vitriol in check as frequently as you can. The good news is that the cruel voice in your head doesn't berate you with the same intensity all the time. It is loudest when you find yourself in situations that make you feel unworthy and low in confidence. Keeping your eyes and ears open to these situational triggers will help you maintain the presence of mind necessary to help your dragon to take a chill pill.

TURN DOWN THE VOLUME

Acknowledging what the voice in your head is saying, however cruel, is an important first step in reducing the power it has over you. I always suggest giving the voice in your head a name that helps take the concept out of the land of theory and into the land of the living. Many of the women who attend my workshops like the term *Debbie Downer* (you know, like the morose, woe-is-me *Saturday Night Live* character). Arianna Huffington, global entrepreneur, mother, and founder of the *Huffington Post*, refers to her voice as her "noisy roommate," and as I mentioned, I'm a big fan of "bitch radio."

The volume and intensity of the negative voice in my own head has come and gone throughout my life. At different points, she has not-so-subtly insisted that I'm not only a terrible mother, but also a dreadful wife, friend, sister, daughter, employee, boss, exerciser, pen pal, and organizer. (Okay, that last one is not true. I'm a fantastic organizer, a real neat freak—and she knows it.) The point is that I'm not immune to what you're going through. In fact, the other day, I came across an old journal where I used to write down the musings from my negative self-talk—an exercise my therapist suggested for me to come to terms with how I was treating myself. And right there, in my own handwriting, were the words *You're a poor excuse for a strong woman.* Maybe you've said something similar or want to stop yourself before you ever do. Either way, what I know is that true healing begins when you're brave enough to start saying that shit out loud.

During my workshops, I invite attendees to contemplate, write down, and share the last terrible thing they said to themselves. I'll never forget when Tina, a mother of one, had the courage to share her response with the crowd. I recognized Tina because she was wearing a fun orange dress that I wished I owned, and earlier in the session, she had acted as an emcee for the event. She kicked off the workshop by proudly telling everyone she'd come up with the idea of the workshop after reading one of my blogs. Then she introduced me and my credentials to the women in the room and sat down. I was happy that Tina volunteered to go first for this exercise, because I was curious to hear what this attractive, talented, and clearly ambitious woman would have to say about herself that wasn't glowing.

In front of 150 working mothers and without missing a beat, Tina said, "The last terrible thing I said to myself was *You did a horrible job introducing Katherine. You suck and everybody knows it.*" There was an audible gasp in the room. I invited the group to respond, and they immediately told Tina that orange was *definitely* her color, she did an excellent job introducing me and, oh, by the way, initiating the whole freaking workshop in the first place.

It did make me wonder what exactly Tina's expectations were for introducing me. Her task was to read my biography out loud. Was she thinking her job was to make my bio *better*? Maybe she was planning to do an interpretative dance to bring my work experience to life but then chickened out? Her job was to do just what she did, and she did a wonderful job. But as mothers who constantly battle dragons, we can't seem to let an opportunity to make ourselves feel like crap pass us by.

After Tina realized the voice in her head was spouting lies while everyone else was telling the truth, the other mothers were eager to share their own mental chatter. "You're not smart, and you've always been behind in life because of it," said Karen. "You're fat, and it's a miracle your fiancé loves you," said Monique. And the astonishing "That's right, keep eating sugar until your unborn baby gets diabetes" from Danielle after chomping on a Tootsie Pop earlier that morning.

We're talking about a *lollipop*, people. The mothers in the room didn't have to go back very far into their mental archives to find a crowd-pleaser. Every single example came from that very same day, and it was only ten o'clock in the morning.

Later in the workshop, the mothers collaborated to see what they could learn from everyone's collective cruel thinking. They determined that the life lesson they wanted to implement moving forward was: *You have to acknowledge the cruel things you're saying to yourself before you can stop them.* Beautifully put. Now, let's get right to it for you.

HOW DO YOU TALK TO YOURSELF?

In order to bring your negative self-talk out of the darkness and into the light, I like to use two different exercises. The first one is similar to the assignment above, and the second will show you just how differently you speak to yourself versus how you speak to those you nurture and love. Together, they'll provide the evidence you need to show that the fuel behind your cruel commentary is not the challenges in your life but your own self-doubt.

EXERCISE 1

What's the last terrible thing you said to yourself? Jot it down here:

....

....

When you see those words, is it safe to say that your dragon is playing DJ? As hard as it might be to read what you've written, think about what your children, best friend, or even your own mother would say if they knew how you speak to yourself. And would you ever say such a horrible thing to another mom or loved one? Now, let's see how the voice in your head would respond to someone you love.

EXERCISE 2

Respond to the situations below. For each hypothetical situation, I'd like you to indicate how you'd respond to yourself versus a friend who found herself in a similar situation.

Situation: You yelled at your son last night. I mean, *really* yelled. What you'd say to yourself:

....

....

What you'd say to a friend:

....

....

Situation: You skipped the gym. Again. What you'd say to yourself:

....

....

What you'd say to a friend:

....

....

Situation: You promised you'd watch a movie with your partner after the kids were in bed, but you fell asleep at 8:35 p.m.

What you'd say to yourself:

....

....

What you'd say to a friend:

....

....

In this second exercise, what can you learn from your responses? What's the key difference between how you speak to yourself versus the people you respect and have a desire to lift up during tough times?

THE REAL MOMMY WARS

Every time I hear women vocalize the horrific commentary that pumps through their veins, I'm convinced all over again that everyone has the age-old wars between mothers wrong. The media loves to write about the "mommy wars," but the truth is, we are the real saboteurs. Mothers are not at war with other mothers; we are at war with ourselves. It's easy to say the war is between stay-at-home and working mothers, between *tiger moms* and *attachment moms*, but that's just tacky clickbait compared to the personal war that's brewing deep beneath your surface.

We are the casualties of this war as we rip ourselves apart all day, every day. And you know what's so ironic? As mothers, we're *terrified* of our child being bullied or, heaven forbid, bullying someone else, yet we bully ourselves twenty-four hours a day and think absolutely nothing of it.

In fact, I often hear women dismiss their self-cruelty by saying things like "Oh, you know me. I'm always my worst enemy" and everyone in the room giggles. But that's not funny. That's terrible! The next time you're tempted to utter a similar phrase, consider what you're actually saying: your greatest enemy in the world is you. We toss out this sentiment like it's worth a two-drink minimum at a comedy club, but it's not even remotely funny. If you want to pave a path to greater inner peace, you must learn to be your own greatest advocate and not your greatest enemy.

INTERNALIZING THE NEGATIVITY

What's astonishing to me is that when the cruel voices in our heads are giving us a real tongue-lashing, we don't turn a deaf ear. We don't tell the voices to shut up; *we listen.* In fact, we believe, trust, and hang on every last word. In his 2017 book *The Untethered Soul,* author Michael Singer discusses our devotion to the negative voices in our heads in an illuminating way:

> *How would you feel if someone outside started talking to you the way your inner voice does? How would you relate to a person who opened their mouth to say everything your mental voice says? After a very short period of time, you would tell them to leave and never come back. If someone followed you around and said to you what you say to yourself, you wouldn't make it past lunchtime.*

He's so right! We'd never last a day listening to someone else talk to us the way we talk to ourselves. Even more upsetting is that we're doing more than just listening to negative thoughts about ourselves; we're *absorbing* them. The traumatizing non-truths you tell yourself nestle into your mind and negatively affect the filter through which you see the world. They affect your decisions (*I should definitely stay up until one o'clock in the morning making a Halloween costume because that's what good mothers do*) and create fears about the future (*My daughter's going to forget my name if I keep spending this much time at work*). Words carry energy and vibration just like anything else in the universe, which means they have influence beyond what you can see or even imagine.

Japanese researcher and author Masaru Emoto thoroughly, and somewhat controversially, studied the power of words for years. As an alternative healthcare physician and healer in Japan in the 1990s, he was intimately familiar with the transformative relationship between energy and water, based on the results he'd experienced with his patients. To prove his point, Emoto placed cooked rice (due to its high water content) in two separate jars. One was labeled *Thank You* and the other *You Fool*. The samples were left in an elementary school classroom where the children were instructed to speak the words on the labels to each jar for thirty seconds twice a day. At the end of thirty days, the rice labeled *Thank You* had not changed or begun to decompose. It looked like the day it was put in the jar, while the other sample had shriveled into a black mass.

If this is what bad vibes can do to water and rice, imagine what they're doing to your body. In other words, if you think you're immune to the detrimental side effects of mean self-talk, remember that the average human body is made up of 60 percent water. So basically, you're not.

IT'S TIME TO CHANGE THE NARRATIVE

One of the reasons so many mothers blindly listen to the negative voices in our heads is that we mistakenly believe that because the voice is on the inside, it's on *our* side. It's a logical assumption. I was there for a long time too. After all, the voice doesn't sound like your strict mother or mean third-grade teacher, but exactly like *you*—with the same stressed-out and exasperated tone you use when asking your kids to pick up their shoes for the nine hundredth time.

Your cruel inner voice is your worst enemy, and it's making life harder than it has to be. To make changes, you need to hear, trust, and believe the following statement with every bone in your body: *You are not the voice in your head.* It might sound like you, but it is not you; it might be inside you, but it is not rooting for you. It is fueled by your dragon, and therefore, it is fighting *against* you. The negative voice in your head is an overly dramatic interpretation of what's going on in your life, as told by the most fragile parts of your ego. It's a collective chorus of the insults and pain that sprang to life the day your dragon was born, and its echoes have reverberated and gained strength ever since.

Knowing that the voice is not who you are also helps you resist the temptation to judge yourself for having or listening to this voice at all. When it yells at you for overcooking spaghetti—*Why in the world can't you ever get dinner right? Is it really that hard to feed your family?*—the last thing you want to think is *Ugh, here comes that stupid voice again. Why can't I keep it quiet?* If you go down that path, it will turn into a never-ending game of *it said, you said*, which might make you crazy for real. The voice isn't stupid; it's the most frightened and anxious part of you telling stories to remind you that you were rejected once and you'll be rejected again.

However, the sooner you realize that you are not the voice in your head, the sooner you can detach yourself and get on with life.

And when you start getting on with your life, make sure your realistic expectations are in check. We talked about expectations in the last chapter, but it bears repeating in this context. Your bitch radio turns up the volume when you don't tame your expectations. *I told you so!* it says. *I told you that you couldn't make PTA president/run a marathon/ host Thanksgiving, you knucklehead.* The more you expect of yourself, the more permission you have to dislike yourself for not delivering. To combat this downward spiral, drown out the voice by setting more realistic expectations for yourself—the more achievable your expectations, the more frequently your mind will stick to critical instead of cruel thinking.

I wish the solution to silencing your bitch radio was as easy as following the age-old advice *If you don't have something nice to say, don't say anything at all*, but it takes more effort than that. Awareness is a big part of this battle. It might help you to imagine your dragon grumbling nasty words in the corner of a dark room. What would happen if you shined a flashlight right in its eyes in the middle of its ugly rambling? You'd startle it, signal that it's time to stop, and it would shut up, that's what.

Here are some tips to help you start curbing your self-criticism and making room for the self-compassion that's coming your way.

* **Acknowledge it's happening.** Have you ever been so swept up while watching a horror film that you temporarily felt like you were *in* the movie rather than watching it? Frightening, right? Similarly, the drama in your head

can become so intense that it sweeps you into its plot even though the story is entirely fictional. If you're able to catch yourself during the movie, you can tell yourself, *It's just a movie. It's not real.* I'd like for you to do the same thing the next time your dragon tries to suck you into its theatrics. As soon as the story starts, say to yourself, *It's a story. It's not me.* The moment you realize that you're not *in* the story, that you're observing it, your dragon will quickly retreat.

✱ **Stay present.** Negativity quickly turns nasty when you're worried about the past or terrified about the future. Time travel is so damaging because it uses everything you should have done yesterday and will inevitably screw up tomorrow to get you going. Moving forward, do your best to keep your thoughts focused on the present tense, what literally is in front of you. For example, if you defrost pork chops then forget about them, try thinking, *Oh look, the pork chops are rotten* as opposed to *Ugh! Why didn't I check the date on the pork chops when I bought them? I'm such an idiot. Now, what are we going to eat tomorrow night? Cereal? Because that's an acceptable thing for a mother to serve for dinner.* Keeping your thoughts in the present tense will keep the cruelty from coming up.

✱ **Direct it toward a friend.** If you're really getting a lashing from the cutthroat voice in your head and able to acknowledge it but not stop it, one final tactic is to direct the voice toward a friend, just like you did in the chapter's earlier exercise. The second you hear your bitch radio's harsh words, pause and kindly ask it to rephrase in a way that is appropriate to say to your mother, sister, daughter, or best friend going through a similar situation. Just because she already said something cruel to you doesn't mean you can't ask for a quick do-over with more pleasantries and manners.

THE TRUTH DOESN'T HAVE TO HURT

Nobody but you can silence your negative voice, because nobody else can hear it. And what's great is that it might not be as hard as you think. Deep down, you know what the voice is saying is *not* true. You know you don't really suck, you're not an idiot, and you certainly know you're not a poor excuse for a mother. If you want to find true and lasting inner peace, the kind that lights you up from the inside, get the truth under control. You're better than you're allowing yourself to be.

The further you separate yourself from the dragon that lurks within, the more apparent and accessible your greatness will become. When you quiet the noise, you'll become a more genuine, kind, and compassionate version of who you've been all along. And when you're able to see the starring role you play in your own happiness and your family's life, you'll no longer need to keep this battle hidden behind a mask. By shutting your bitch radio down, it will be easier to honor what you know—that you're truly amazing and you deserve all the respect, compassion, and love you have to offer.

TELL YOUR MIND TO *zip it.* YOUR SOUL HAS SOMETHING TO *say.*

CHAPTER 6

You Posture Like a Pro, Then Wonder Why Nobody Sees Your Pain

*A*ll moms are guilty of putting on a pretty face and stretching the truth to an extent, at least in the heat of an awkward moment (say, to a math teacher during conferences: "We definitely practice long division *every night…*"). Who doesn't sit up taller to make themselves look and feel a little bit better? However, if you believe you are broken and that you must hide that brokenness to be liked, loved, accepted, or admired, then your dragon is going to encourage you to take your fibs further than they need to go. You'll become prone to putting on a mask. This is a facade that says *I'm more than enough* on the outside as you silently tell yourself *I'm nowhere near enough* on the inside.

The difference between fluffing your feathers a bit and posturing to the point of putting on a mask is the intention behind your efforts. Posturing is designed to build on the good that's already there, while wearing a mask is about covering up the bad you *believe* is there (and likely isn't). When the women from my research studies find the courage to dig deep and pinpoint why they're hiding their truest selves, it's often because they're terrified that others won't accept them if they have flaws. The day their self-doubt began to creep into their lives, a sense of rejection and isolation cut deep, hurt bad, and left some nasty memories behind. So, they hide their doubts, fears, and flaws behind a shield of armor to prevent anything like that from *ever* happening again. In other words, to keep rejection about as far away as the bubonic plague.

I know about facades all too well, because I clung to my own for two decades. I put on a mask and held on to it like it was my lifeline, because it *was* my lifeline—a dirty secret that saved me from exposing my struggles. It kept me from having to confess, "I'm working eighty hours a week while shouldering household burdens, and it never feels like I'm doing enough. I feel like I should be doing more, but if I do anything more, I might keel over." If I shared how I felt with a friend, my husband, or a coworker who could help lessen the load, I was terrified they'd think less of me, and even the *possibility* of that outcome made me want to vomit. The promise of approval and affection was like an oasis to my dehydrated soul—it kept my need to feel worthy alive.

My need to please was relentless, and my mask offered me an opportunity to try to attract love from those around me, because it was nowhere to be found inside me. My strategy to parade around like I was perfect was a desperate attempt to encourage my insides to catch up to my outsides. I assumed that if I pretended everything was okay, eventually, it would be. Fake it till you make it, right? Not this time. I assumed that, at some point, my inadequacies and insecurities would magically attract the joy that I projected to my own parents, children, bosses, strangers, and neighbors. I believed my mask would get me there faster and with less pain.

But the mask produced the opposite effect—the more I wore it, the more my insides diverged from my outsides. The more under control I pretended to be, the less in control I felt. The more success I chased, the less fulfilled I was when I achieved it. And the more I pretended that motherhood was easy, the harder it became. My mask helped me in the short term, but it hurt me in the long run. It eventually split me in half—successful on the outside, suffering on the inside. This double-life dynamic mirrors a dysfunctional parent-child relationship where the nasty parent, or in this case the mask, says, "You're embarrassing me with your problems, so you just sit in the corner and keep your mouth shut, and I'll do the talking."

In this chapter, I'll help you face when and why you wear your mask, to the point of telling bold-faced lies. Recognizing that you're wearing a mask is the first step toward ripping it off and never putting it on again. The day will soon come when you admit that you're a grown-up and playing make-believe is for children, when you derive your self-worth from yourself, not other people, and when you love yourself more than you love impressing other people. We'll tackle learning to love yourself in chapter 10, but for now, let's start by getting a peek behind that mask of yours and at the beautiful person hiding behind it.

ARE YOU POSTURING OR LYING?

We banish our children into time-out when they don't tell the truth, but apparently, more than a few adults should be sitting on a stool with their nose in the corner. Consider the study "Lying in Everyday Life" that researchers published in the *Journal of Personality and Social Psychology* in 1996 after conducting an experiment in which 147 people from ages eighteen through seventy-one kept diaries of all the untruths they told over the course of one week when interacting with others. Most subjects, they found, lied twice a day—almost as often as they snacked from the refrigerator or brushed their teeth! Both men and women lied in approximately one-fifth of their social exchanges lasting ten or more minutes, and over the course of a week, they deceived about 30 percent of those with whom they interacted one on one. Makes you second-guess all the small talk in the carpool line, right?

Interestingly, when examining the reasons that study participants bothered to lie in the first place, they found that three out of four falsehoods were "self-oriented." In other words, the lies were designed to protect the person telling them by reducing guilt, embarrassment, and shame, or increasing self-esteem, affection, and respect. It's what psychologists call *impression management*, or, as I like to say, blowing smoke to make yourself look and feel better in front of others.

Take comfort in the fact that you're not the only one playing Pinocchio, but please, for the sake of your future inner peace, don't pooh-pooh the idea of making meaningful change in this area by saying, "This is not a big deal. All moms lie to make themselves look better. No need to change my ways." Take it from someone who studies the lives of mothers every day—that statement is *not* true. All moms posture; some moms lie.

Posturing occurs when you edit or exaggerate a true statement— like when your son's jungle-themed bounce-house birthday party is fun but also incredibly exhausting, yet you only rekindle the fun parts when updating your mother. To me, standing a *little* taller and making your life look a *little* better is more like putting on makeup than wearing a mask. It's still your life and your truth—just with fewer blemishes, wrinkles, and bags under your eyes. All moms do it. And according to my research, nobody gets hurt.

Lying, on the other hand, involves the deliberate fostering of a false impression, like when your partner's anger issues are ruining every fleeting moment of family time, but you tell your girlfriend that everything is "excellent" at home—like it's nothing. But it's *not* nothing; it's a covert cover-up operation, and they come in all shapes and sizes. Maybe you tell your mother that you don't need help at home when you're barely sleeping four hours a night. Maybe you tell your girlfriends you're too busy to start dating again when, really, you're terrified you're not dating material. Or, perhaps, you give the impression that climbing the corporate ladder is a dream come true when it's the most soul-depleting activity you've ever taken on.

The distance between the truth and your lies is where the pain exists—the bigger the gap, the more frequently fear and friction show up and put a frown on your face. The pain from wearing a mask doesn't originate from lying to others. In a strange twist of magical thinking, it comes from lying to yourself. While others might not know you're wearing a mask, you know you've got one on. And every time you lie and say "I'm fine!" when you're not, at its most basic, you are being dishonest with yourself. You're saying to yourself that you value what someone else thinks of you more than you value the truth—your own truth.

If you want to move from fear to freedom, the difference between posturing and lying cannot be confused. If you're bypassing the makeup and reaching for a mask, your motivation isn't to supersize your strengths to appear *more* perfect, but to hide your inadequacies to avoid looking or feeling *less* worse. Well, it's time to come out of hiding. Beginning today, start paying close attention to your social interactions when you feel the tendency to hide, stretch, or tell the truth. Awareness of your current behavior will go a long way toward curbing it in the future.

SIGNS YOU'RE WEARING A MASK

As you start to become a witness to the stories you're telling, keep an eye out for three major indicators that a cover-up operation is at play.

1. You answer most questions twice—once in your head and once
   out loud. When your colleague asks how your vacation with two
   young kids went, your instinct says, *It was horrible. I couldn't wait to
   get back to work*, but a nanosecond later, your mouth says, "It was
   fantastic. Who doesn't love the beach?" When your sister asks
   how potty training is going, your internal response is *He still hides
   behind the sofa to poop*, but your external response is "He's rocking
   it! The kid's a whiz—no pun intended!" This is what I mean by
   your mask splitting you in half—at times, it can feel like you're
   leading a double life. Dragons love it when their host mom starts
   seeing and saying double, because all your remaining energy after
   cooking, cleaning, and wiping everyone's tush goes to battling
   your truth, not your dragon. And it gets to live another day (insert
   evil dragon laugh here).

2. Your conversations are a real snooze. Have you ever found
   yourself talking to a friend and consistently using insanely boring
   adjectives like *great, amazing, awesome*, and *wonderful* when she asks
   how you're doing? The conversation doesn't go far, does it? If
   you weren't wearing a mask, you'd be more likely to say, "I feel
   good, minus the fact that I'm exhausted from work and my son is
   being a punk lately," and then you'd have a far more interesting
   and meaningful conversation.

3. When everything you're taking on and covering up becomes too
   much, you get pissed off because others don't notice or offer to
   help. But *hello*, they can't support what you don't show them.
   When your mother rolls her eyes because you ordered takeout
   instead of cooking for your family, it makes you want to shake

her and scream, "Can't you see that I have fourteen projects at work, eight homework assignments to supervise, six friends I haven't talked to in a year, three children to feed and bathe—all before 9:00 p.m., and it's already six o'clock?" But you don't say that because it will give you away and make it look like you've lost control. So instead, you internally seethe. Take the mask off, and you'll undoubtedly feel the same relief that Blake, a mother from one of my workshops, experienced when she admitted, "Wow. When I stopped hiding my broken bits, life got infinitely easier."

YOUR MASK-WEARING WAYS

It's not an easy thing to admit that you wear a mask. Frankly, I found it harder than persuading my husband to move from his native Switzerland to America and avoiding doughnuts when I suffered from gestational diabetes. If it makes you feel better, my research shows that no mom puts on a mask in the morning and wears it all day. Most just flaunt their faux flawlessness to certain family members, colleagues, moms on the playground, or circumstances in which they feel insecure, inferior, or threatened by potential rejection. For example, Meghal, a mom of two from India who participated in a round of Opinion Parties with The Mom Complex, said that she's able to let down her guard at her own mother's house, but it's a completely different story at her in-laws' house. She works herself into a froth cooking, cleaning, and caring for the kids because she's scared her mother-in-law won't think she's good enough for their most cherished son. (This isn't the first time I've heard this.)

So how does your mask show up in your life? Take a moment to consider:

WHEN DO YOU WEAR A MASK?

When do you find yourself pretending to be something you're not? What aspects of your life are you fearful about feeling exposed?

....

....

....

....

....

WHY ARE YOU WEARING IT?

What are you trying to prove in those situations or in front of those people? What are you trying to demonstrate, protect, or hide from?

....

....

....

....

....

Living one life is hard. Living two lives is a bitch. If you've been keeping quiet because you simply don't want to burden people with your problems, I want you to rethink that assumption. It sounds legitimate enough, but in my experience, it's more of an excuse for a mother to take on too much, smile when she really wants to cry, and never ask for help. It's an excuse to once again dodge the question *why?* Why do you think others will feel burdened, and if they truly are, why do you allow them to have starring roles in your life? Why do you let them behave as accomplices to your dragon's dirty work?

EFFECTS OF WEARING A MASK

Masks might help you look polished and pretty close to perfect on the outside, but behind the scenes, they do some real damage to your body, mind, and spirit. This is a trifecta that I want to help you strengthen, not continue to weaken.

On the physical front, when your mask suggests that nothing is wrong and everything is awesome, you end up distancing yourself from the help you rightly deserve. As a result, you end up cooking all the meals, signing up for way too many school activities, and skipping the gym to run errands for your son. In other words, you wear your ass out and rarely allow others to step in and assist. Helping hands and supportive greeting cards that say *Girl, you got this* belong to women who are courageous enough to admit they need them. As mothers, we *all* need these things; we're just not all willing to do what it takes to get them. Meaning, be honest.

Masquerades also wear out your mind. When you know something to be true—that your job is deflating your soul, your marriage is on the rocks, or you cry yourself to sleep at night trying to figure out your son's new food allergy—but you say *the complete opposite* is true, two parts of your brain go to war with each other. According to Columbia University researcher Michael Slepian, one part of your brain called the cingulate cortex wants you to tell the truth. When that doesn't happen, another part of your brain, the prefrontal cortex, kicks into overdrive, imagining all the negative consequences of holding onto this secret. Then, when the truth-seeking part of your brain loses the battle and a lie is told, it ramps up the production of stress hormones that negatively impact your memory, blood pressure, gastrointestinal tract, and metabolism. And you thought the crummy results of your latest physical were simply from the frozen pizza you keep eating off your kids' plates.

Sadly, the greatest shame in your mask-wearing game is that you're cutting yourself off from love. Hiding your doubts, fears, struggles, and screwups prevents your true self from being seen and therefore loved. You've adopted the belief that the rules of love are predicated on always being a fantastic friend, wonderful wife, supportive mother, and doting daughter. However, there is no greater love than when you show someone your busted and brittle bits, and the look in their eyes says they love you just as much, if not more. Being admired for pretending to have your act together is *nothing* compared to the depth of love that shows up when you feel fully seen.

I want you to experience the true, unabashed, unconditional love that's already coming your way, but your self-doubt is blocking you from seeing and accepting. Just remember that your silence will not help you get there; only breaking it will.

ARE YOU GIVING YOURSELF THE RUNAROUND?

Despite putting your back into parading around as someone you're not, the truth is your mask isn't going to get you where you want to go. Even if you achieve your goals and win over everyone in sight with your ability to manage a job, family, house, and international conference calls, it *still* won't be the love you're longing for because it will come from the outside, not from within. Proving yourself to others will never salvage your self-esteem. Trust me, I've tried. I made it to the top of a massive pile of praise, which was *exactly* what I wanted. However, all the external love and respect in the world couldn't save me because I knew it was in celebration of the fake me, not the real me. I found out the hard way that those kinds of accolades are valued at only slightly more than worthless.

In my case, everyone could see the success I'd gained, but nobody could see the motivation *behind* the success—that I wasn't simply working hard to be good at something but working relentlessly *to be seen* as good at something. And, therein lies the truth. The mask is not a vehicle for you to appear more put together in the eyes of other people—you have makeup for that. The cover-up is a conduit for self-love, i.e., if other people approve, respect, and love me, then maybe, just maybe, I will approve, respect, and love myself again. And off we go again: performing, perfecting, and pleasing our way into the hearts of others, ultimately with the hope of winning over our own hearts along the way.

Here's an idea: What if you just loved yourself? What if you supported, respected, and admired you just for being you, and anyone else who loved you felt like icing on top of an already beautiful cake? That's what my self-love looks like today. But this is only because I poured all my frustration, exhaustion, and fatigue into shattering my mask into a thousand little pieces to make sure I'd never be tempted to hide behind it again.

LOOK AT (THE REAL) ME

You'll know you're ready to take off your mask when you start mumbling thoughts to yourself like, *I can't keep up this charade; I'm too tired to keep moving at this speed; This is bullshit.* I started uttering these statements (and other profanities) when I realized that others liked me, but I still didn't like myself. My energy to run two separate lives was officially depleted, and I decided that I needed help more than I needed the world to think I was perfect.

I peeled my mask off slowly—allowing my true feelings to slip out a little at a time—and I suggest you do the same. In one-on-one conversations with friends, family, and even strangers, I admitted I was tired, overwhelmed, and far from perfect. However, to my surprise and disappointment, my truth was often dismissed before it was even digested. A colleague belittled my cry for help by pointing to my "charmed" upbringing and how grateful I should be. A close friend responded, "You? Unhappy? With all that you have, I can't believe it." And my personal favorite, which made my blood boil, was "Don't be silly, Katherine." I always thought, *Don't be silly?! I just said some really scary shit out loud, and you think I'm making a joke?*

As one of my favorite mom crushes and *New York Times* bestselling authors Glennon Doyle Melton says, "When you're skinny and you smile a lot, people think you have everything figured out." Yes, they do. It finally dawned on me that when you're an actor on the stage and people like the performance, it's very hard to get off the stage and out of that character.

Eventually, I decided that I needed to stop relying on others to validate my new sense of self (I was basically doing what I'd always done, only in a different way) and found the most public place possible to stand up and say, "Here I am, world, full of flaws and all. Take it or leave it." I spent six months writing, rewriting, and laboring over a poem that exposed every ounce of my tired soul at a TEDx conference in Richmond, Virginia, with five hundred people in the audience and thousands watching online. Here's what I recited to the crowd:

I'm not June Cleaver.
I'm not Claire Huxtable, Elyse Keaton, or Carol Brady.
This is not the story of a lovely lady.

I don't dance around my house in cardigan sets and capris.
Clearly, I don't have perfectly coiffed curls…and I've never
cleaned a toilet bowl in high heels and pearls.
My days are spent washing and brushing, cooking and cleaning, feeding
and fussing and "Don't lick the dog!" Driving and dropping, racing and
rushing and "Holy shit I'm tired!"
And it's only 9:00 a.m.

But, I saw moms on TV—happy and free.
I saw moms on my street—perfect and neat.
I saw moms on playdates wearing makeup and smiles sixteen-teeth wide.
And I sighed.

As I sat in my recliner…covered in drool, urine, vomit, and last night's
chardonnay. Those were the mothers I saw and declared: "There is no
way." "We are NOT the same kind."

I said this in my mind.
But with them, I just smiled and lied and said: "Everything's just fine."

I thought I was joining a club. A group of like-minded souls.

So why was I the only one totally out of control…while everyone around me carried on like Shirley Partridge on performance-enhancing drugs?

So, for years, I wore a mask—thick, bold, porcelain, beautiful.

Desperate to impress other people because I was so unimpressed with myself, and happy that no one could see me cry, allowing others to turn a blind eye to a life built on other people's expectations. I started wearing other people's faces.

*And when I looked in the mirror, I saw what others saw—
a big, bold smile that said to the world Look! I'm happy!*

*But on the inside…I was kneeling at the altar of the voices in my head—
the all-consuming, all-annoying voices that said I wasn't good enough.
Not patient enough, smart enough, nice enough, tough enough, calm enough, thin enough, wife enough, daughter enough, sister enough, and God knows, I wasn't mom enough.*

*I wore the mask, smiled, and said, "Everything's just fine."
But everything was not fine.*

*Who were these women? I needed to know.
What did they know that I didn't know?
All I knew was that everything I knew
couldn't possibly be all there was to know. You know?*

So, I asked. I came from behind my mask and I asked.
Not one mom, not a few, but five thousand seven hundred and eighty-two.
From Shanghai to Seattle and seventeen countries in between.

A nerdy researcher by trade, these questions became my crusade.
I gave them tools to dig deep down inside.
To better understand their Jekyll and my Hyde.

You know what that neighborhood of motherhood revealed once they removed
their masks? No one feels up to the task. "We are not what we pretend to
be." From Shanghai to Seattle, mothers everywhere—just like me.

Burdened with doubt. The number one emotion of all was the doubt.
They doubt whether they're doing a good job at this most important job.
And they're unable and unwilling to say anything when they feel like
they're doing a bad job.

It's a code of silence. Crying in silence. Suffering in silence.
Voices in their heads suggesting that as a mother what they should be,
could be, shouldn't ever be, and couldn't be…even if they tried.

The media loves to write about the mommy wars.
But the truth is, we are the real saboteurs.
Mothers are not at war with other mothers; we are at war with ourselves.

You see…how we feel about ourselves,

what we do to ourselves is a condition of our own creation.

Just think of the world we could create if we created a different situation.

We wear masks because we believe we must.

It looks so easy for them, so we say it's easy for us.

But it's not easy for any of us.

And we're making it harder by trying to live up to ridiculous

expectations and all these fictitious motherhood rules and regulations.

We can only ever be who we really are…and at some point,

that has to be good enough. Let's agree to agree and come to the conclusion

that we are good enough.

Let's find the courage to be who we really are, say who we really are,

and accept who we really are. And together, we can end the mommy wars,

the wars within ourselves, and finally be free.

I didn't drop the mic when I was done because it was one of those Madonna-looking headsets attached to my face, but I definitely dropped it in my mind. To date, the talk has been viewed tens of thousands of times across twenty-two countries, and I regularly receive letters and emails from mothers who felt their own mask strings loosen as they watched me come out of hiding, embrace my imperfections, and finally take my life back.

With your mask off, you will feel increasingly comfortable verbalizing the good, bad, and ugly, until eventually, you no longer need the mask at all. The key word here is *verbalizing*. If you keep your perceived inadequacies a secret, or only find enough courage to scribble them down in your journal, you will never experience the sheer joy, excitement, and relief of realizing they were only perceived that way by you. Because masks are about hiding, saying you're struggling or flawed out loud will cut a clear road to redemption and healing. You thought you had to be perfect to be loved, but being flawed and seen will bring you more joy, love, affection, and support than you ever knew possible.

TAKE IT OFF, BABY

You don't have to strip down in front of thousands to free yourself from your mask's restraints, but you do have to find the courage to be truly you—in all your messy, real, and raw glory. Your sleepless child, your cranky canine, your crappy boss, and your uncertainty about gluten-containing ingredients don't make you a loser; they make you human. Here are a few suggestions on how to remove your mask and show your true self to the world:

* **Spend quality time alone.** Because you know the truth, but you keep telling other people lies, start spending more time alone than you have in the past. Take a thirty-minute walk without listening to music, drive the long way to work and just breathe, or lie on the bedroom floor and tell yourself it's time to be done with the charades.

* **Find an audience.** Begin looking at every social interaction as an opportunity to tell the truth or a repeat lie. You might be thinking that strangers have no interest in listening to your baggage, but those are *exactly* the people I want you to start opening up to. Remember the magical moment I had with the security guard in my office? She asked how I was, and I said I was tired. She said, "Me too," and we hugged it out. I'm not talking about channeling Jim Carrey from the movie *Liar, Liar* and telling people about your sex life or how attractive you think your friend's husband is. I'm suggesting that when others ask how you're doing, you respond with a quick truth. You'll be training your brain to take the honest route, and you'll start receiving more support in return.

* **Give yourself a pep talk.** Once you've identified the people and circumstances for which you're most likely to wear a mask, before entering testy situations, repeat the mantra *real me in real time*. This will help keep you honest when you're tempted to fluff your feathers or reach for your mask to make yourself look or sound better.

PERMISSION SLIPS ACCEPTED HERE

As you begin to take off your mask, don't feel weird or weak for relying on permission from other people to do so. You don't *need* permission from anyone. I'm just saying that if you get it, go with it. My incredibly supportive boss could see my mask long before I even knew it was there. Late one night as I was polishing off yet another project, he looked past the bags under my eyes, right into my soul, and asked, "When are you going to stop trying to prove that you deserve to be at this dance?" And as you know, my husband single-handedly sparked my self-help journey by posing the game-changing question, "What's so wrong with being you?" Both were provocative questions that not only gave me permission to start showing my true colors to the world, but also required a soul-searching journey to uncover some decent answers.

I've heard the same from other moms—that more often than not, someone gave them the permission they needed to stop hiding and start fully being seen and loved. Maybe this book will be your source of get-up-and-go, or maybe it will be your sister, friend, colleague, or child's science teacher. Regardless, when they give you the push you need, don't push back. Use the extra wind in your sails as positive momentum to move forward with life as *you* want it to be.

WHEN YOU PUT *half-truths* INTO THE WORLD, YOU FEEL *half-loved* IN RETURN.

CHAPTER 7

You Compare the Way You Feel to the Way Others Look

I'll never forget when I first met my friend Kat, a former lawyer turned stay-at-home mother to three. Kat used to be my husband's mixed-doubles tennis partner, and when our husbands proposed a double date for us to meet, both of our self-doubting dragons had us *convinced* that the evening would end in rejection. The doubt in my own head said, *She's a great tennis player, and you barely know how to hold a tennis racket.* I found out later that the voice in hers said, *That woman has a job, owns her own company, and wears pants with a zipper every day instead of elastic. Good luck striking up a conversation with her.*

My research has shown that when other moms excel, it can be a major trigger that makes you feel anxious, nervous, and self-conscious. The comparison game you're playing—and more often than not losing—is little more than a desperate attempt on behalf of that monster inside you to make you feel different, and inferior, to the moms around you. Kat and I, for instance, were two women needlessly worrying about meeting each other, because as we quickly found out, dancing to eighties music and sipping vodka tonics would be our tie that binds—not our tennis game or desire to work outside the home. All those fake shortcomings, and their imaginary rejections, only existed in our heads; once we were in the real world, our score was love–love.

What Kat and I continue to realize, and what my workshop attendees learn to see, too, is that honesty and vulnerability are the best solutions for putting your self-doubt to sleep and moving from inferiority toward self-acceptance. In this chapter, I'll explain how defeating and unnecessary the comparison game is, and why you'll be happier when you groove on past it.

HEALTHY VERSUS UNHEALTHY COMPARISONS

At some point, every mother has compared herself to another mother. Apparently, it's human nature to do so. In 1954, psychologist Leon Festinger proposed the *social comparison theory*, which claimed that people determine their social and personal worth based on how they stack up against others. It makes sense, then, that you would look at those with similar characteristics (i.e., other mothers or women who somehow remind you of yourself) to compare yourself with. You're less likely to compare yourself to a sixty-five-year-old male billionaire who lives on a yacht in the Indian Ocean (although, you might stack up as a better mother if you did).

Not all comparisons are created equal, however. If you look to those who do things better than you in order to learn from them—like getting cooking tips from a girlfriend because you couldn't boil an egg if you tried—that's a healthy comparison. You're okay with where you fall short, and perfectly happy finding someone more experienced to help fill in the gap. It's important to note, however, that healthy comparisons are only possible when you feel neutral about both your abilities and inabilities. Because if you think your cooking skills are letting yourself, your family, and humanity down, then your comparisons will quickly become incredibly unhealthy. Suddenly, watching your girlfriend whip up eggs Benedict with hollandaise makes you think you don't just suck in the kitchen, you suck in general. When you're starting from the deficit of doubt, comparisons are no longer an opportunity to learn, but an opportunity to browbeat yourself into feeling like half a human.

Comparisons come in two forms. The first is what psychologists call *upward comparisons*, in which you stack yourself against people you perceive to be doing a better job than you at (you name it) and when you pale in comparison, you feel like a chump. Like when another mother brings a homemade quiche to Teacher Appreciation Day, and you bring a bag of chips and a jar of salsa. *Downward comparisons*, by contrast, involve belittling the circumstances of others, which help you feel better about yourself. In other words, you make these comparisons to give yourself a lift when you feel bad, and in doing so, you remind yourself that at least you've never been divorced like Devin, fired like Michelle, married to a jerk like Naomi, or to rehab like Adrian. For the purposes of this chapter, we're going to focus on upward comparisons, because they occur more frequently among moms, do significantly more damage, and give your dragon entirely too much ammunition to attack you.

While some moms can look at others doing great things and either blow them off or think, *Huh, that's cool. I need to learn from that woman,* moms who suffer from self-doubt immediately feel *She's amazing. I need to hide from that woman (and maybe the rest of the world while I'm at it).* The thing to realize when you're tempted to get lost in comparisons is that every mom has different gifts, circumstances, and support. And when you compare their best to your worst, you don't give yourself a fair shot at being equals. It's like when you ate your friend Polly's amazing homemade tuna tartare and flashed back to when you made brownies with olive oil instead of vegetable oil, and immediately began ticking off all the other areas that Polly rocks and you fall short. Imagine how much better you'd feel if you paused on only one thought: *That's incredible tuna tartare—just as good as my chicken pot pie. I'll have to get her recipe.* I bet you'd like her, and more importantly yourself, a lot more.

EYES WIDE OPEN

Typically, there are two categories of mothers you're using for upward comparisons as you compare, compete, and complain your way toward more anxiety and less self-compassion. The first group is the mothers who are personally present in your life. Because you're regularly exposed to them, it's likely that you're watching what they do and then—here's the catalyst that starts sinking your ship—wishing you could do it better. You tell yourself, *Okay, lady, if you can't be as good at this gig as you'd like, then at the very minimum, maybe you can be better than the other mother in front of you.* The problem is, your habit of grasping for any self-worth in sight by outdoing someone else doesn't help you come out on top. When the limits of your time and frankly your ability cause you to fall short, your bitch radio starts blasting *Let's just go ahead and put an L-squared next to that showdown—for loss and loser.*

It should come as no surprise, then, that your triggers become the mother who dropped her pregnancy weight in three weeks or the mom at the swimming pool who sees her seven-year-old son nearly drowning her toddler yet gets him to stop in a very even-keeled voice. It could even be as simple as your neighbor who manages to wash her hair every day. Despite the fact that you're a grown woman, when you're around these moms, your dragon of self-doubt turns you into an insecure mean girl back in middle school. And yes, just as middle-school showdowns seem silly in retrospect, eventually, you'll realize the same is true with trying to show up, down, and off around other mothers. That day will come when you develop enough self-compassion to realize motherhood isn't a competition.

The second group of moms who feed your dragon are those you're watching from afar. These moms aren't in your daily orbit, but they can certainly cause your confidence to dip lower than a teenage girl doing the limbo to impress an older boy. It's the mom blogger and social media maven you follow who must live in some kind of time warp, because there's no way she gets so much done and still exercises every day, or the Emmy-winning actress who seems to have the best job, life partner, children, and shoe collection on the planet. Or it's the overly fit, overly charming woman who gave the keynote speech at the last conference you attended who seemed so put together while you were slouching in your seat, stuffing your muffin top into your skirt, and kicking yourself for even packing a skirt when you hadn't shaved your legs in two weeks.

Your goal in the comparison challenge is to get to the point where you look at other mothers, both near and far, not as women to compete with, but as comrades in the hardest but most rewarding job in the world, moms with whom to share your highs and lows. For true growth to occur, start focusing less on what *they're* doing and more on how *you* feel when you walk away from each encounter, because that's the feeling you have to live with. Recognizing that you can control the circum-stances that elicit those feelings or at least alter how you react to them can help you enter each mom encounter with a calmer head. Eleanor Roosevelt is quoted as saying, "No one can make you feel inferior without your consent."

WHAT'S THE AWARD FOR WINNING?

It's a well-known and unfortunate fact that motherhood is considered one of the most competitive sports around. Even if you grew up competing on nights and weekends in national softball, gymnastics, or tae kwon do championships, you ain't seen nothin' until you've shown up to a preschool bake sale, kindergarten back-to-school night, or a Saturday morning swim meet and witnessed mothers trying to one-up each other. In an era when all kids get a trophy for participation, it seems that it's the mothers who so desperately want to walk home with a shiny gold symbol of how much better they are than women who are supposed to be their teammates. Yet when we're constantly comparing ourselves to and competing with other mothers, what *exactly* are we trying to win?

Danielle, a participant in one of my workshops, recently answered this question for all the moms in the room. With a level of fatigue and exasperation that's typically reserved for those who run marathons and come in last place, Danielle explained how tired she was from comparing herself to other moms and then running herself into the ground to pull off heroic parties, perfect brunches, thoughtful teacher gifts, and impossible shenanigans with her Elf on the Shelf. When Danielle limped over the finish line of her story, Robin, a young mom with the demeanor and wisdom of a Buddhist monk, raised her hand and kindly asked her, "What are you trying to win?" Taking a big gulp, Danielle pondered her answer while looking down at her feet, up at the ceiling, then out into the room, and finally said, "Self-respect, I guess."

And that's the truth, my friends. Comparing ourselves to other mothers and competing for fictitious accolades, titles, and heroic hoopla is yet another desperate attempt to feel good enough, prepared enough, nice enough, and of course, mom enough. While every mother participates in more comparisons than she'd like to admit, this dynamic can be particularly challenging if you're already fighting feelings of inadequacy in any category—at work, in your marriage, you name it. Fathers, by the way, don't participate in nearly as many competitions over imaginary parenting credentials. And grandparents? Forget about it. Those people are all heroes.

Maybe it's time to cut yourself a little slack.

WHY DO YOU COMPARE YOURSELF TO OTHERS?

Comparing yourself to other mothers causes you to walk on eggshells around *all* mothers in a constant state of wonder about what constitutes not enough, good enough, and entirely too much. Your dragon keeps you on your toes, dancing to a mantra that sounds a lot like *Don't try too hard or you'll look like you're trying too hard, don't take the path of least resistance or everyone will think you don't care about your kids, and definitely don't order that third glass of wine or you'll look as intoxicated as you wish you actually were.*

Deep down, you know this is an exhausting way to live, but according to my research, there are three reasons you keep on keeping at it. First, you see yourself as separate and therefore different from other mothers. But you may not be as different as you think, at least from a scientific perspective. Did you know that your DNA is a 99.9 percent match to the mother you feel less than because she never yells at her children? It's crazy but true!

Long before the mommy wars were ever documented, Albert Einstein dropped some truth on this topic by insisting that our feelings of separateness are an "optical illusion of consciousness" that can feel like a prison at times. The only way to free ourselves from these perceived differences is to see ourselves as one. I often tell my workshop mothers to hit pause on their tailspin of comparisons and take an imaginary trip to outer space for a little perspective. If you were an alien and visited Earth to observe the women who made and raised the humans, wouldn't you conclude that they had more commonalities and shared experiences than differences? Exactly—because we do. Remembering that, as mothers, we're all on the same planet, with very similar DNA, plus similar wishes, hopes, and dreams for our children, will go a long way toward not seeing other mothers as magically more equipped or better than you.

The second reason you participate in these games is because self-doubt has you operating from what's known as a *scarcity mentality*—a zero-sum mindset that says there's simply not enough good deeds in motherhood to go around—and that's a very fearful way to live. If Allison does something amazing, you worry she's siphoned up some of the rationed *Good job!* tokens and now there aren't enough for you. Dragon-fighting moms often derive a sense of self-worth by comparing themselves to other moms and attempting to come out on top. So when Allison does something stellar and sucks up the accolades, her success means your failure, because she beat you to the punch. That is to say, if people think she's great, they can't possibly think you are, too, because in this warped reality, only so many moms can be amazing.

The final force encouraging you to constantly look over your shoulder is the metaphorical authority figure that goes by the name *They*. Blindly following the wisdom of this nobody begins after giving birth and continues until, well, you stop it. And it sounds like this: *They say you should breastfeed for at least the first year; they say boys should start kindergarten when they're older; they say you're ready to have sex six weeks after giving birth…* If you believe there's one right way to be a mother, then you'll constantly keep a scorecard of who's keeping up and who's falling behind (namely yourself). I always say that it's never a good idea to let someone you don't know—and, in this case, *doesn't even exist*—be a driving force in the decisions you make as a mother. Your decisions should be determined by and dependent upon your body, your mind, your child, your goals, and your desires. Period.

NEVER ASSUME. IT MAKES AN ASS OUT OF YOU AND…WELL, MOSTLY YOU.

The biggest problem with making comparisons is that you compare other mothers at their best to you at your worst. Any chance this scene looks familiar? Thirty seconds after walking into another mother's house and noticing how tidy it is, you jump from fact to fantasyland where the other mother is a hero and you're nothing but a trash fire. You tell yourself that if she can find ten minutes to pick up before a guest arrives, then she *must* also be an amazing cook, have sex with her husband every night, and feel no pain when she steps on Legos.

While you fantasize over your friend's fictitious life, the

fire-breathing dragon in your belly that's burning up your insides whispers, *She's perfect, and you're pathetic.* None of those hypotheses you've made about the mom or your dragon's response are true, of course— they're optical delusions. They all stem from the ultimate presumption that other mothers have this operation on autopilot because you can't fathom that anyone finds this job as hard as you do.

What's really a crying shame is that when you determine that another mother is fabulous and you're crap, you then begin to question her motives for being so awesome. You needn't look any further than two mothers green with envy over another mother's Pinterest talent to see this phenomenon in action. The one phrase I hear most often is "I mean, you just know she's doing that shit *on purpose!*" When comments like these come up in my workshops, I often interject by inquiring what exactly one believes that mother's purpose is—to ruin their lives by making them feel like the worst birthday party gift bagger that ever lived? The answer is always the same. "Um, *hello?* Yes!"

Know this: At The Mom Complex, we've studied the craftiest Pinterest mothers around, and they are not posting to piss you off; they're doing it because they like to make stuff with their hands. Their passion stems from many self-preserving, resourceful, and humble places—an escape from their incredibly dull day job, a useful skill they mastered to make money when they were broke, a hobby they learned from their own mom, or simply an alternative to watching TV. I won't bore you with all the other reasons I've heard (I'm sure the ones you've made up in your mind are a hundred times more interesting, devious, and clever), but rest assured that *none* of them have *anything* to do with sabotaging your sanity.

When you make assumptions, you set yourself up to suffer. My advice is to start paying attention when you're tempted to make a leap— between Emma's ability to make a mean meatloaf and her ability to balance a checkbook, or Paula's underlying motivation for building the best Pinterest board you've ever seen. It is a choice, and a mistake, to see someone else making different choices and assume those differences are somehow a direct criticism of you.

Consider what author Don Miguel Ruiz writes in his 1997 bestselling book *The Four Agreements*: "We have the tendency to make assumptions about everything. The problem with making these assumptions is that we believe they are the truth. We could swear they are real... We make assumptions, we misunderstand, we take it personally, and we end up creating a whole big drama for nothing." In other words, we confuse our perception with the truth. And unfortunately, right now, your perception of other mothers is a direct reflection of your self-doubt: the less you think of yourself, the more you exaggerate the strengths of others. It's a dragon's dream come true. While you're running around collecting evidence that you're unworthy of love, respect, and pats on the back, your dragon maintains control of your life. Assumptions are nothing more than lies you tell yourself, and you sell yourself and your relationships short when you use them to influence the world around you.

People make assumptions about me all the time. Because I run a successful company, they assume I've never struggled or sacrificed as an entrepreneur. Because my children speak French, they think I'm fancy, when it's really because my husband is from the French-speaking region of Switzerland and I don't want the kids to feel like losers when we visit his family. And I often share the story that when

I was named Working Mother of the Year by the Advertising Women of New York, I sent my husband and children back to Virginia on the train and I stayed to party with my girlfriends, dance on coffee tables in nightclubs, and down entirely too many tequila shots. Looks can be deceiving.

Okay, now it's your turn. Take a minute to complete the exercise below by writing down a time you made an assumption about another mother that turned out to be false, plus an example of one that others might make about you that isn't true. For example, Elizabeth, one of my friends, shared that because she's very well read, everyone she meets assumes she grew up in a rich and privileged household. But as she tells it, "I didn't read books because we were rich but because we were so poor that we didn't have a TV." See what you come up with:

An assumption I made about another mother:

....

....

....

An assumption others make about me:

....

....

....

ÜBER-MOM...OR CYCLOPS?

When it comes to comparing yourself to others, it would be one thing if you admired your sister-in-law's ability to get a thank-you note out on time and felt inclined to improve in just that one area of your life. But, that's not the case. If you're like the mothers from my research, you want to clean better like Karen, eat better like Mary, rise to the ranks of partnership like Maria, read more like Charlotte, and discipline your kids better than your own mom did. You don't want to be a better mom. You want to be mutant mom—to take the best trait that each woman has to offer and use them to create an über-mother, the kind of woman who exists only in science fiction. And there you go, working tirelessly to achieve this crazy ambition until you collapse in a pile of mental and physical exhaustion in the middle of folding laundry (and it's nothing like the way Beth folds laundry…).

When your goal in life is to become an über-mom, you might appear put together on the outside, but you're sending a strong signal to your soul that the life you're currently leading isn't good enough— that you're not good enough. And slowly but surely with every wish from the list you just completed, you're building a case against self-compassion. Once you learn to accept yourself, flaws and all, then you'll learn to love and appreciate yourself for who you are now, rather than who you need to become. When that happens, how other mothers choose to spend their time will become about as meaningful as an episode of *SpongeBob SquarePants*.

The goal of becoming an über-mom is typically an attempt to be perfect. But when you stop and think about it, is perfection *really* what you want? My research says it isn't. In 2013, I conducted a study with five thousand mothers across the country and asked two questions: *What kind of mother are you today?* and *What kind of mother would you like to be?* The metric was simple: plot your answers on a scale of one to five, with one being the worst mother and five being the perfect mother. The average answer to the first question was 3.5. Well done, Mamas. You consider yourself better than average. Surprisingly, though, when it came to the second question, not a single mother in the entire study said she wanted to be a five. No one wanted to be the perfect mother. When I inquired as to why, one mother said, "Because we hate those bitches."

I get it. It's human nature to dislike perfect people, and it's why most of us would rather have a glass of wine with Monica Lewinsky than Martha Stewart. Right now, what you're really longing for is permission to take on less because it's all too much, and the fictitious five in my research study make you want to vomit because people like that, whether real or perceived, make it hard to lower the bar to a realistic level. My advice? Stop trying to be the bitch you hate. Think about your friends. How many are perfect? None. How much do you love them? A lot.

LEAVE THE KIDS OUT OF IT

One of the most dangerous side effects of comparing yourself to other mothers is that the habit begins to feel so natural that it extends to other areas of your life, most notably comparing your children to other children and practically losing your mind over it. All mothers naturally want to make sure their kids are crawling, walking, and reading at the right age and stage, but some moms take things a step further by transferring doubts about themselves (*I'm royally screwing this up*) to doubts about their kids (*I'll surely screw them up too*).

What's interesting is that The Mom Complex was once hired to help a major toy manufacturer launch a new line of toys for mothers of preschool-age children. The clients were convinced that labeling and promoting the toys by ages and stages (i.e., crawling, standing, walking) would help moms know which products to buy. However, our research revealed that *even the idea* of someone's child not aligning with what was on the packaging (six to twelve months/crawling) caused way too many mothers to see the discrepancy as a personal indictment. In the end, the marketing platform was released without any recommendations for when a child would be ready for the next stage, allowing moms to figure out the timing for themselves instead of worrying about fitting in and falling short.

Children hit milestones at different times, and as mothers, we do the same. So, comparing ourselves to other mothers and our children to other kids is never quite as meaningful as we think it will be. No two kids are alike, and no two moms are alike either. We think we're comparing apples to apples when it's more like apples to bologna sandwiches.

BREAK THE HABIT

While comparing yourself to others has become part of who you are, it's a habit you need to break if you want to stop feeding your dragon. Paying attention to when you compare and contrast yourself is the first step toward catching yourself in the act and seeing the truth for what it is. Here are a few ideas that can help support you in that process.

* **Change your social media feed.** If scrolling through all the picture-perfect images on social media gives you more anxiety than the thought of walking down the street naked,

shift who you follow. You get to decide whose perfection shows up on your phone and how it makes you feel. Until you master the art of ignoring it, you might need to escape from it.

✱ **Ask your friends to open up.** When you start thinking that everyone has life figured out and yours is the only one filled with trials and tribulations, get others in on the honesty game with you. When having lunch with a girlfriend, ask her, "What's the hardest part of motherhood for you?" When grabbing a cup of coffee with another mom at work, ask her, "Is your life as a working mother as chaotic as mine?" And when looking for survival strategies, ask another parent, "What's one thing you're doing to make your life easier these days?" Honesty begets honesty, and the more you see others revealing their truths (even when they're forced), the less you'll put them on the pedestal of perfection.

✱ **Practice, practice, practice.** Avoiding the temptation of comparing yourself to other moms takes practice. If you want to get better at it sooner rather than later, and you're already signed up to take a beginner yoga or painting class, go out on a limb and change a reservation or two to an intermediate class. Everyone in the class will clearly be more experienced, and you can use these opportunities to train your mind to think, *Wow, they're good*—without taking it to *and that means I'm terrible.* Learning to check yourself in one context will help you apply it to other scenarios.

BRINGING IT HOME

Someone once said, "Comparison is the thief of joy," and I believe that wholeheartedly, because I've been on the giving and receiving end of many comparisons and false assumptions. If you want to compare in order to learn and grow, that's always a good idea.

However, shadowboxing assumptions that aren't true is a complete waste of time during a period of your life when time and self-love aren't exactly sitting around in excess.

From time to time when I need perspective, I interview mothers in their eighties. I ask them what advice they would give younger moms to avoid all the stress and pressure that come with raising happy and healthy human beings. The other day, Betty, who's eighty-nine years old, a mother to four, a grandmother to eight, and a great-grandmother to nineteen, shared these wise words: "Keep your head down, get the job done as best you can, and forget about what everyone else is doing." If that's not sage advice, I don't know what is.

If we're blessed enough to live to our eighties, I think we'll all be saying the same thing. So, why not start saying it now?

IF YOU DESPISE *"perfect"* mothers, THEN STOP TRYING TO BE THE BITCH *you hate.*

CHAPTER 8

You. Just. Can't. Say. No.

*A*s mothers, we say yes more often than we should. It's a hazard of the job. Maybe you say yes to other adults when you're new to the party (e.g., in a new school, relationship, or job) and want to fit in by being a little overly agreeable and available. Perhaps you also become a yes-woman to your kids when after a long day of negotiating meals, homework, and tube-top selections, you simply don't have the energy to fight anymore. Or if you're having a rough go as a single, newly divorced, or working mother, the guilt you feel over saying no to chaperoning school field trips might tempt you to say yes to more toys, TV time, and ice cream to make up for it.

None of these situations are ideal of course, but your intentions behind them are relatively clean. They're conscious decisions to say yes, particularly during taxing times, and I don't suggest losing much sleep over them. You've got bigger fish to fry, and they're a relatively quick fix once you become aware of them.

Your time and energy will be better spent focusing on the situations when your intentions are a little more wonky—when your motivation is to impress and persuade, or when you say yes because you're desperate for everyone to believe you're capable of carrying the world on your shoulders. You can detect these situations because that double life of yours shows up again. You know, when your next-door neighbor invites you to yet another fund-raising event, and your intuition says,

Please, for the love of God, decline this invitation; I'm exhausted, but your mouth says, "Are you kidding me? I can't wait. Can I bring a cheese tray?" It's likely you're saying yes because you're longing for others to love you and doing more for them feels like a fast pass to making that happen.

In this chapter, I'll help you see that you're giving away your precious time because you believe others deserve it more than you—and that needs to stop. To quiet this self-sabotaging habit, I'll help you shift your perspective from worrying about who you're saying no to and toward thinking about who's on the receiving end of yes—not just you, but all the people who your newfound happiness and calm will touch. Through this proven process, you'll be able to take your time *and* power back and start showing that dragon of yours who's boss.

FACING YOUR FEARS

You might tell yourself that your plate is full because you're too qualified, selfless, or too nice to say no, but that's not the real story; it has nothing to do with a self-possessed generosity. In fact, if you ever checked in with yourself while filling in your oversized dry-erase calendar for the month, you'd realize that all this yes-ing makes you feel like the exact opposite of confident and sane.

At the heart of your *I'm all yours* mentality is a deep-seated concern about letting others down, which you might have done in the past and may be linked to what birthed or has fed your dragon over the years. For instance, you don't have to spend years in therapy to realize that when you disappointed your parents growing up, all hell broke loose. Now that you're a grown-up, it still triggers a worry that the same could happen if you let down a teacher, child, boss, friend, or homeless man playing guitar in the subway. What's more, as if the pressure you put on yourself isn't enough, our society values women who "do it all" by calling them strong, putting them on magazine covers, and celebrating their ability to multitask. However, while others may see strength in a woman who does everything for everyone else while running on four hours of sleep, if you are this woman, we both know it's a weakness.

I'm not diminishing the value of hard work—it is important to work hard to achieve big things that are meaningful to you. But does offering to run yet another bake sale when you're also juggling sports schedules, a sick parent, and a big work assignment *really* qualify as meaningful? When you reach the finish line, will your blood, sweat, and tears lead to what you're longing for, or will you just be a bloody, sweaty, and tear-stained version of your former self? If you're looking for self-love, respect, and compassion, it will never be found by giving away your time and saving nothing for yourself. Instead, start choosing who gets a piece of you, and how big that slice is, so you have more of you for yourself and for the things that truly matter.

WHO'S GETTING THE BEST OF YOU?

How often have you found yourself painting a kid's face at a fall festival or playing pin the tail on the dirty diaper at a baby shower for a colleague you hardly know, and you think to yourself, *What the hell am I even doing here?* When you don't feel good enough about yourself, this scenario happens a lot—which, believe it or not, has a positive side. That astute observation is your intuition trying to protect your already scarce time and energy by making a mental note that you should have said no. The good news is that this means you're having moments of awareness that require attention, and when those moments happen, you need to seize them. If your soul is telling you *Enough is enough*, then it's time to start listening. If your mind and mouth ignore these prompts from the deepest, truest part of you, you are basically signaling back to your soul that other people deserve your time more than you do.

I also believe that if you liked spending time by yourself and felt you deserved to be taken care of, you'd make me time a bigger priority. You'd set aside more time for girls' nights and less for Girl Scouts, and you'd stop pulling all-nighters at work to start pulling them with your partner. You'd also get there not by wishing for more hours in the day, but by refusing to give so many away. I often hear mothers say, "But, but, but...my parents/children/church/clients/dog/boss/neighbor needs help!" I have no doubt they do—everyone could use an extra pair of hands. But don't *you* need help too? And most importantly, why does your mouth keep giving away what your soul is begging you to keep?

What's also dangerous about saying yes too often is that beyond bounce-house birthday parties and carpool lines, conceding to others can change the trajectory of your life, and you may not even realize it's happening. If your dragon is calling the shots, you're not making conscious choices; you're a hamster on a wheel, mindlessly chasing activities and signs of appreciation with no end in sight.

Did you hear the one about the reality show contestants who agreed to spend one year living out in the isolated Scottish wilderness tending livestock, building their own shelters, and eating gross bugs for a show called *Eden*? Four weeks in, several of the contestants thought, *This sucks; I'm better than this*, and quit the show to return home to running water, real food, and warm blankets. The remaining contestants pushed through misery only to find themselves in increasingly difficult, compromising, and dangerous conditions. There was bullying, cliques, fistfights, animal killings, anger, and misogyny. The contestants were not in control—they chose to put their happiness and health in a network's ratings-hungry hands. At the end of 365 days, they returned home to find out the show had been canceled after airing only the first four episodes.

At some point, I'll bet each and every one of their own souls told them *Enough is enough*. But they didn't listen either. And it was all just a massive waste of time and sanity.

Like these aspiring TV star bug eaters, a life spent repeatedly saying yes while ignoring what your instincts are shouting is not conscious living and will set you up for a rude awakening. One day, you will wake up to find yourself in a career or marriage, or shouldering responsibilities, that make you so miserable, frustrated, and exhausted that you lie in bed at night *wishing* you could live in the Scottish wilderness with a bunch of strangers for a year just to get away from it all.

So much of my life is the perfect example of this. When my dragon was at its most powerful, I had fifty ways of saying yes, including *you got it, I'm all over it, I'm in, I'm all yours, you can count on me*. At the time, I told myself that my actions allowed me to convey *I want to help you, I care about you*, and *you matter to me* to others. Yet, the truth was, it was never really about altruistically helping others. It was about wanting to prove what I was worth, to them and to myself. That's not what an outstretched hand should be about, so it backfired. The more I helped others, the more I hurt myself, until I woke up living a life filled with disgusting junk food three meals a day, no form of physical exercise, and literally no knowledge of current events—like the time a hurricane hit my city and took me by complete surprise. It's only now, with my dragon dead and gone, that I realize that for every action—like saying yes to others— there was an equal and opposite reaction—saying no to my own needs, desires, and apparently safety. And you can't be on the losing end of that physics lesson for too long without collapsing.

PLUG UP YOUR HOLE

If you want to regain your time, energy, and self-assurance, you'll need to figure out how to fill your proverbial bucket. Despite pumping your bucket (a.k.a. your life) full of activities, accolades, and attaboys, you still feel empty inside—like something is missing in your life despite the tremendous blessings that surround you. Why? Because your bucket has a hole in it caused by the belief one that you've chosen to uphold—that you're not whole or good enough as you are. Therefore, the solution to finding and maintaining a deep sense of fulfillment isn't to keep putting *more* stuff in the bucket, but to plug the damn hole by *deciding* you're a worthy human being and therefore deserve rest, relief, and relaxation. When you adopt this perspective, you'll find that less is more. You don't need external approval via sixty-two busybody activities and accomplishments in a single week. You need internal approval, which will come when you start believing you're good enough as you are, stop saying yes to ridiculous requests, and begin effortlessly filling up your bucket with experiences that actually matter.

A word of caution here. If you decide today that your job is wearing you out and you blow into HR tomorrow and quit, be very careful about replacing your tendency to overextend yourself at work with overextending yourself at home or your kid's school. In that case, you'd still be operating from the top of the bucket. For real change to happen, you must believe that you are enough when your soul says *Enough is enough*. You don't need to stand on a pile of accomplishments to know, trust, and believe that you're a good human being.

This reminds me of a woman I know named Amelia, a young mother of two and one of my blog followers. Amelia's dragon was born when, as a young girl, her mother, who didn't go to college and therefore relied on her husband's income for the family's financial security, repeatedly told her, "Make sure you're independent enough that you never have to rely on a man!" Amelia actually credits this mantra (albeit fear-driven) for what helped motivate her to become a successful director for a hedge fund in Manhattan—and it's probably not a coincidence that she chose to take on a notoriously male-driven world in an I'll-show-you style. She commuted three hours to get to her office, which created a sixty-plus-hour workweek that left no time to recharge or hang out with her kids. Her fuse was always shorter than she wanted it to be, as her stressed-out brain was in constant fight or flight. And she worried that if she even thought about turning down opportunities at work or asking her husband for help, she'd be a disappointment because strong women don't depend on men. So Amelia poured even more activities into her bucket, never plugging up the hole in the bottom to feel happier and more fulfilled, all so she could prove her merit to everyone else and feel good about herself in the process.

When you're overextended, however, and you don't listen to your soul, your body will sound its warning—yet another example of how your mind, body, and soul work as one. Heart palpitations, fatigue, funky hormones, even brain fog are all signs of a body crying uncle. In Amelia's case, she blacked out on the train platform, face-first, after her train pulled into New York City. As Amelia jokes, "Have you been to Penn Station? I must have been near death to let my face touch that floor."

Amelia was immediately rushed to the hospital and diagnosed with a heart condition, which forced her to reclaim her life and fix the root of her problems or else worsen her illness. She did this by allowing her husband to help out, expanding her nanny's duties, and going to therapy, meditation, and yoga.

Not only did Amelia allow herself the space to get her health under control, but her family grew closer and she began to listen to her instincts when she took on too much. She also realized that nobody cared about the fact that she was saying no as much as she thought they would. The world kept spinning, so Amelia kept saying no until she eventually found the courage to tell her boss she wanted to work from home two days a week so she could swap her commuting time for time with her children—and he agreed, so long as she got her work done. And, boy, did she. Later that year, Amelia's boss noted on her performance review that she seemed happier and her productivity and work product had improved.

Saying no didn't look, feel, or smell as selfish as Amelia thought. It ended up being better for everyone involved.

YOUR TURN: LEARN TO SAY NO

So, how can you learn to say no and mean it?

First, I want you to invoke the opposite of the Golden Rule, which says to treat others the way you'd like to be treated. If you're a people-pleasing mom, then this rule essentially suggests that you could get away with treating other people like shit. So, when learning to say no, I often suggest reversing the Golden Rule and suggest this mantra instead: *Treat yourself the way you like to treat others.* It's a real win–win, if you ask me.

Saying yes when you really want to say no isn't some personality flaw you're born with—it's a learned behavior. Picture how your mother responded when, as a young child, you said you wouldn't put on your socks, eat what she made for dinner, or clean up the stick figures you drew on the dining room table. She probably banished you to your bedroom to rethink your defiant ways. By the time we reach adulthood, it's no wonder so many of us suffer anxiety at the thought of saying no. You'll have to fight against this most basic instinct as you grow.

Like most habits that feed your dragon, your inability to say no is born from fear and panic. *Will my boss give the highest profile assignments to the coworker who says yes to everything? Will not participating in the bake sale hurt my daughter's chances of fitting in at school? Will it hurt my son's feelings if I don't have time to help him?* The good news is that because you're *deciding* to layer fear on top of your decisions, you can decide to stop doing it as well. And when you do, you'll see that the fear you feel isn't real. It's a lot of smoke and mirrors put in place by your dragon to freak you out.

One way to start diverting your dragon's spiteful ways is to start prioritizing what matters most to you as a mom. In the exercise on the following page, list five things that fall into this category—we'll call this category the major league. These should be things that deserve your time because you believe in them. For example, consistent family dinners, annual family vacations, advancement at work, memorable birthday parties, kids getting good grades, or having a healthy relationship with food. Next, make a note of what *shouldn't* be on the major list. Not that these items aren't important; you just can't major in everything. Examples from my workshops include serving as the class mom, dressing your kids to the nines, and going to the gym six days a week.

MAJOR LEAGUE

The battles I want to win	Why they matter	What does winning look like with these activities?

MINOR LEAGUE

The battles I'm willing to lose	Why they're less important	What would deprioritizing these activities look like?

Setting priorities is the first step toward drawing boundaries and getting some of your life back. We fall into exhaustion when we assume all activities in our life are created equal. They're not. I started finding free time all over the place when I had the courage to say things like, "I can't do it all, so volunteering at my son's school is a battle I'm willing to lose." What did you learn from your own classifications above? Are you ready to put these priorities into action?

SETTING BOUNDARIES IN ADVANCE

One of the simplest ways to start saying no is to prepare ahead of time for the most obvious encounters that will need to solicit a big fat no from you. Figuring this out early will also take some of the anxiety out of feeling like you're constantly surprised by sneak attack requests.

During awkward moments when an ask hangs in the air, my favorite suggestion is to picture the person asking you to do something you don't want to do as a teenage boy trying to make out with you. Pretend you're still a teenager and imagine the offender as a handsy and mildly audacious pile of hormones who has one goal in mind—to take all he can get and still ask for more. Maybe it's because I made out with too many guys in high school, but seeing all these askers as randy dudes works for me every time. To this day, when someone asks me to do something that might jeopardize my boundaries, I think to myself, *I'm not going to make out with you right now.* Then I giggle, put my foot down, and say, "Not gonna happen." Try it the next time you're in a position to overextend yourself. Eventually, you'll get so used to how good it feels to call your own shots that you'll start setting boundaries before the heat of the moment so that you don't have to deal with these so-called mauling teenagers. You'll no longer have to wait until your boss begs, "But we need you at this meeting in LA on Thursday!"

Setting boundaries in advance lets you off the hook in the future. That might mean telling your sister-in-law that Sunday brunches are wreaking havoc on your kids' nap schedule and you're indefinitely out, coming clean to the coach that you can't serve as a timer at any more swim meets, or confessing to your neighbor that you'll see him at church but you no longer have time to volunteer on a committee. It's important to speak your truth aloud because you're more likely to protect what you hear yourself say, especially knowing that others heard it too.

If you're a working mom, letting your boss, coworkers, and team members know if you have standing events far in advance of when they occur will keep the sweat from forming on your brow when you need to shuffle out of the office early for ballet lessons or sports practice. What's interesting is that my research shows that working mothers struggle with this guilt-ridden issue more than dads. In fact, when I ask parents to draw on a piece of paper what happens when they walk out the door from work early for a kids activity, dads literally draw a stick figure walking out a door. Moms, however, go for a more colorful approach such as sketching dozens of floating eyeballs that watch them as they sheepishly slink out a side exit.

So, when it comes to standing appointments, it's not a bad idea to turn to dads for advice here. I'll never forget one of my events when Naomi, a working mother of three very sporty kids, said she couldn't bring herself to ask her boss if she could go to her son's 6:00 p.m. baseball games every Wednesday. Instead, she silently promised herself she'd go but then got caught up at work and stayed behind to be a team player.

Naomi found it hard to voice what she cared about and didn't feel she deserved the time off if she also expected to climb the ladder at work. Hearing this, a father suggested she reevaluate her approach and ask permission for the entire baseball season, not one game at a time. Even though Naomi had been angling for a raise, she channeled the chutzpah she'd need to say to her boss, "Baseball is important to my son, so it's important to me. I'd like to know if it's okay to leave every Wednesday at 5:30 p.m. for the next eight weeks to be there for his games." Naomi held her breath for fear of being judged or rejected, only to find an understanding boss and father seated across the desk from her. His response? "Of course you can. Let me know how the season goes."

I WANT YOU TO WANT ME

To get serious about saying no more often, you'll need to stop taking yourself so seriously.

Your dragon of self-doubt has you so convinced that you're a poor excuse for a _____ (insert any major role in your life) that you lean on a curious coping mechanism for getting your mojo back that plays into your need to say yes all the time. To put it bluntly, you like to hear other people say you excel in that role *so much* that your services are always truly and deeply needed and appreciated. According to author and psychologist Harriet Braiker, "To please is a disease," and, in excess, it can become an addiction that eventually results in neglecting your own health, happiness, and sanity. When you're asked to save the day on a project at work or host a neighborhood cocktail party, it feels good, because what you hear is that you're *so good* at what you do, others need your help. You hear the validation you crave. You might even say to yourself, as I'm embarrassed to admit I did for years, *How dare you say no and deny these people your skills and talent? How will they possibly pull this off without you?* Remember when I told you earlier that, deep down, you *know* you don't suck? Thoughts like this are proof that you think you're pretty darn good at what you do. The problem is that hearing from you isn't enough. You need to hear it from other people. And so you agree to take on yet another project because you know that when they thank you profusely, you will feel good that your abilities were recognized and appreciated.

And *that's* what *really* makes saying no so freaking hard. You're not just saying no to chaperoning a field trip; you're saying no to a chance to feel better about yourself. However, the unfortunate truth is that when you *do* occasionally say no to others' requests, the projects still meet their deadlines, cocktail parties still happen, and balloon animals still get made. This might be hard to hear, but this means people don't need your help as much as you hope and pray they do. You surely bring terrific skills to the table, don't get me wrong, but you are not irreplaceable. And, frankly, some of the time, people are just flattering you to get the job done.

Right about now, your dragon of self-doubt might have you wondering, *If I say no and nobody cares, then do I even matter?* If you remember that you're in charge and not your dragon, this notion can be incredibly empowering. The fact that the show will go on without you is liberating. You don't need others to validate your self-worth at every turn by doing everything they ask. From here on out, if any part of you says yes because of what the women in my workshops describe as "feeling like I should," "sensing someone will be disappointed if I don't," or "seeking redemption," your answer shouldn't just be no—it should be *hell no.*

WELL, WHEN CAN I SAY YES?

None of this means you should say no to every opportunity that comes your way—that would be boring. It's about balance, with you calling the shots. Remember your major league and minor league charts? Your goal is to do more that feeds happiness and less that strains it. So go support your children, partner, boss, friends, neighbors, parents, and community, but make sure it counts.

Setting boundaries is critical to living with inner peace and calm. Why? Because the word *no* is the barrier by which you establish and maintain the perimeter of yourself—in other words, where you end and someone else begins. Think of it this way: if you lack boundaries, then you lack defined edges, and your responsibilities, morals, and what you stand for start to ooze out everywhere like that glow-in-the-dark goo your kids get out of bubblegum machines. Setting clear parameters about what you are willing to do (help with math tests, organize sporting activities) and not willing to do (work weekends, fix breakfast for your kids) sends a strong message to everyone around you, and they eventually stop asking. It's the exact message your dragon needs to hear too. It says, *I love, respect, and value my relationships with others, but I will not bend to their will at the expense of myself.*

Of course, not everyone will be hip to your new boundaries. It's one thing to say no to the next PTA meeting, chili cook-off, or origami class at the library, but it's something much bigger to say no to a bad boss, verbally abusive husband, condescending friend, or soul-sucking career. These *I'm done* conversations (and subsequent confrontations) are much harder to muster. The fallout runs the risk of cutting deeper, hurting more, and disappointing others.

A lot of people, possibly including those you love most, are going to be startled over your new limits. Chances are you're going to sustain some losses. When I began telling people I wanted to walk away from my job in advertising for a more fulfilling career path, the fallout came from all sides—horror stories from friends with failed businesses, shame-filled comments about how much "your job has given you," and, point-blank, "I don't want you to do this" from the president of my company, someone I loved *dearly* and who was literally on his deathbed at the time.

These interactions will test you more than you've ever been tested before. People you love, respect, and admire will tell you to not go forward with the *no* you know you need to deliver. After getting all your ugly cries out of the way, the one question you need to answer is *who are you living your life for?* When I walked away from my "enviable" career, I did so in defiance of the advice from my husband, parents, and mentors—the people I loved and trusted most in the world, the people I would have previously done *anything* to impress.

I found the strength to still do it because I made the conscious choice to stop living my life for everyone around me. I didn't know what life would be like as an entrepreneur, but I took the leap anyway, because my heart, soul, and instincts told me there was a better life waiting on the other side. The more confidence I gained in my decision, the more my loved ones got on board. My husband's fear turned to excitement; my parents' worry morphed into pride; and three weeks before he passed away, the world-renowned president of my company mailed me a letter sealed with his blessing: "Any sadness I feel over your departure can, and will, be replaced with happiness knowing that you'll be living the life you want to live."

Saving yourself means having the courage to love yourself, even when you risk disappointing others. What I've experienced and seen repeated thousands of times with other mothers is that when people see true joy in your heart and soul, they come around. They want you to be happy, and if walking away from something monumental makes you happy, then do it—for yourself and all those who will benefit from the joy that waits on the other side.

SAYING NO REALLY MEANS SAYING YES

One of the best ways to motivate yourself to say no, especially if you think it feels negative or selfish in some way, is to shift your thinking away from who's on the receiving end of no to who's on the receiving end of a consciously chosen yes—and that includes you and your loved ones. Saying no to a Saturday afternoon block party could mean saying yes to that nap you've been waiting two years to take; saying no to an exhausting desk job could mean saying yes to fun collaborations that excite you; saying no to a man who doesn't respect you could mean saying yes to deeper friendships and new bonds with others who do.

It isn't always about you, of course. Spending less time tethered to volunteering at the local women's club because all your neighbors do it could translate to more time volunteering at a dog shelter because you love animals or helping your elderly neighbor run errands because her husband just passed away. The point here is to focus your time on what fills your soul with joy and meaning and at the end of the day makes you—and others—have a life well lived.

Let's put a plan in place to help you say yes to yourself more frequently without giving it too much thought. We want this to eventually become an instinctual way of going about your day. Start by taking a minute to jot down below the top six activities that bring you tremendous joy and fulfillment. When you participate in these things—at work or home, with your children or alone—you feel lighter, brighter, more enriched, and more you. Then list the top six activities or factors in your life that drain and exhaust you.

Energizing	**Draining**
1.	1.
2.	2.
3.	3.
4.	4.
5.	5.
6.	6.

Next, pick two activities from the list on the left and put them on your calendar as recurring meetings starting five weeks from now. If yoga and thrift-store shopping with your daughter are on the list, schedule in a few yoga classes a week and a monthly shopping excursion with your youngest. And vow to say no, now more than ever, to the activities on the right.

The reason for starting further out is that finding time for yourself tomorrow is impossible because your calendar looks like your son's colored pencils threw up all over it. There's no room for you in sight, and trying to squeeze it in would be like trying to squeeze into your pre-pregnancy jeans the day after giving birth. Five weeks from now, however, your calendar is nowhere near as full—there's plenty of white space to play with! And guess what? When the future becomes the present, you'll already have yourself and your priorities programmed into your calendar. You'll learn all about living in the present moment in the next chapter, and this life hack is an excellent tip to make sure you'll enjoy every second of it.

Saying yes to yourself will always be a better way to spend your time. And with a stronger focus on yourself, your dragon will increasingly fade into the distance.

WHEN YOU GIVE AWAY YOUR *free time,* YOU BELIEVE OTHERS DESERVE IT *more than you.*

CHAPTER 9

You Forecast the Worst for the Future

*M*others, by nature, are planners. After all, it takes a whole lot of foresight to make sure our kids stay well-fed, safe, and happy. We lie in bed at night running through to-do lists that seem to have their own to-do lists: *Did I pack all the bathing suits and mouth guards for our trip to Florida? Do I have enough snacks for the car? Should I grab extra bug spray in case the mosquitoes are teeming with the Zika virus? Which reminds me, should I ask the pediatrician for her cell in case of an emergency?* We try to prepare for 937 possible outcomes, best and worst cases included. This helps us feel in control of the unknown as much as we can, since—let's face it—who's going to remember all the good stuff that needs to happen to keep the bad stuff away if not a mom?

Some mothers, however, don't simply ready themselves for the future: they constantly throw themselves and their families into a dreaded, imaginary nightmare that's about to happen any second. If your kids don't do their homework, they won't just fail math—they'll be addicted to drugs by age fifteen. If you don't volunteer to run that project at work, you won't just delay a promotion—you'll be fired and humiliated for all to see. And if you eat a doughnut, you won't just feel bloated—you'll get diabetes. If your dragon is calling the shots, when a new situation arises, you freak out and go from zero to sixty in seconds, flattening perspective along the way. You don't prepare or fuss over what *could* happen; you panic because you're convinced that what *will* happen will never be okay. And from that baseline, the monster inside you has you convinced that you must try harder, know more, and do more to stay ahead of whatever catastrophe will occur.

As if you're not already taking on enough.

But (and it's a big but), how many times has your story *actually* ended the way your hyperbolic mind hypothesized it would? Hardly ever, right? Trust me, I know. Disastrous outcomes used to dance around in my mind on the regular, especially at work, because that's where I was looking to prove myself. If a client needed me to travel out of town at the last minute, I would cancel plans I'd previously made—celebrating my husband's birthday, trick-or-treating with my children, drinking wine with my girlfriends—because I could see *exactly* what would happen if I said no. The client would fire my agency, we'd lose forty million dollars in revenue overnight, and 156 people would soon be forced to fight back tears as they told their spouses and children that they no longer had a job. I had that fear-based, dragon-induced scene etched in my mind for years, and guess what? Even when I started drawing boundaries and saying no, nothing even close to that horror show ever occurred. Talk about a waste of energy.

And that's not even the worst part. One of the greatest tragedies of fearing the worst for your future is that you miss out on the good news when your fictional future never comes to fruition. When your daughter aces that test, you get the promotion you were gunning for, and you stay healthy despite your sugar habit, these moments and realities go unacknowledged or are dismissed as good luck, fortunate timing, or a total fluke. You're so busy worrying about the future that when the present moment turns out pretty darn well, you can't even see it.

In this chapter, you'll learn how destructive it is to live in a frightening future and that if you can learn to live in the now, you'll have more energy left over for what's happening in front of you. You'll see that your kids are just fine, and in fact, they're learning to pat themselves on the back when they do well without your anxious hovering. You'll find that when you spend all that time worrying about your husband's devotion, you'll never notice when he looks at you adoringly as you wipe the snot from your daughter's runny nose. And what monumental relief you'll feel when you stop treating the present like it's a means to a disastrous end.

WHAT'S UP WITH YOUR MIND?

If you have a mind that drifts back and forth between what you forgot to do this morning and what you will likely screw up this afternoon, you're not alone. Wondering (and wandering) minds think alike. Psychologists at Harvard University collected information on the daily activities, thoughts, and feelings of 2,250 men and women to find out how often they were focused on what they were doing and what made them happiest. The 2010 study, titled "A Wandering Mind Is an Unhappy Mind," found that subjects spent nearly half their time (46.9 percent) thinking about something other than what they were actually doing. What's more important, and dare I say terrifying, is that the researchers concluded that reminiscing, thinking ahead, or daydreaming tends to make people more miserable. The ultimate conclusion? The human mind is a wandering mind, and a wandering mind is an unhappy mind.

If you're thinking, *Thanks, Katherine. Now tell me something I don't know*, then buckle your seat belt. When I read the international bestseller *The Power of Now*, it really whipped my brain into focusing on the present. Inspired by the wisdom from author Eckhart Tolle, I'd like for you to focus on the present moment—not five minutes from now, five years from now, or five o'clock this morning—and list three problems that you have. Think about multiple areas of your life, not just your maternal side. Use the space below and see what you can come up with.

PROBLEMS

1. ....
2. ....
3. ....

    If you listed concerns like not knowing what to make for dinner tonight, your daughter growing up too quickly, your kids feeling scared by your pending divorce, or a loved one's recent breast cancer diagnosis—that anxiety, stress, and worry represent fears about the future, and they're not actually problems in the present moment. Dinner will happen six hours from now whether you're prepared or not, and your divorce may or may not affect the kids in the way you're picturing in your mind. Similarly, if you conjured up the fact that you pursued the wrong college degree, you wish you'd married your second boyfriend instead of the third, or you ate four brownies for dessert last night—all that guilt, regret, resentment, and bitterness means your mind is recalling problems from the past.

    Neither is productive or healthy. And there isn't a thing you can do about any of them, because you can only deal with the here and now—never with the distant past or possible future. In fact, the present moment is your only point of access to inner peace. It's fascinating, isn't it? In this exact moment, and then again in this one, too, you don't have any problems.

What Tolle taught me and I've shared with thousands of women since is that problems are *mind-made*, and they need time to survive— meaning the past or the future. I like to encourage moms to live in the now as much they can. But, try to suggest to *any* mom that she live in the moment, and she'll probably laugh and tell you that it's a great idea for when the kids go to college. Basically, it sounds like an airy-fairy pipe dream when you're currently working hard to juggle life's details without dropping too many balls.

Here's a quick example of stripping life down to the present moment that might feel familiar. A few years ago, I found myself running late for a tennis tournament. The mean voice in my head annihilated me during the entire eighteen-minute drive across town: *Way to go, Katherine! You're going to be late, get disqualified, let your team down, and prove once again that you don't have your act together. Everyone else manages to show up on time, so why can't you?* After arriving as a hot, sweaty mess and profusely apologizing to anyone who would listen, the captain of my team told me that my tardiness was no big deal because the courts were still occupied, and our team wouldn't go on for another twenty-five minutes. In that moment, I realized what you just realized while reading this: all my energy-depleting smack talk was totally and utterly unnecessary. I discovered Tolle's powerful life lesson about living in the present moment later that same week, and I was immediately able to see the error of my ways and reduce the number of times it happened moving forward.

The thing is, while I was driving to the match, I technically had no problems. If you remove the recent past (I lost track of time) and the doomsday future (I was going to get disqualified), the present moment was, well, just what it was. A moment in time when I was driving my car down clean and safe roads, blessed enough to have a healthy body and supportive husband, both of which made it possible for me to play tennis on a sunny Sunday afternoon. End of story. If I had remained in the present moment instead of fast-forwarding to the future, I could have listened to my favorite podcast, counted my blessings, and waited to see what the future had in store for me when I arrived in *that* moment. And the truth is, even if I had been disqualified, there would have been zero upside worrying, stressing, and fretting about it in advance.

I suggest the following exercise in my workshops: if while brushing your teeth and putting on makeup in the morning, you're tempted to block, tackle, prevent, and get ahead of fourteen disasters that'll surely happen by noon, simply say to yourself while staring at your reflection, *This is it. This is the goal. Brushing my teeth is the endgame.* Then move on to the next moment in your day, such as making breakfast, and believe that moment is the endgame as well. Because the only thing that's real, that's not perceived, is the event that's happening *right now*. Once you get more practice under your belt, you'll soon see that a ticking clock fuels a lot of your pain, and to be free of that is to be free of a past that you view as the source of your inadequacies and a future that's riddled with failure.

THE FUTURE, NOT THE PAST, IS THE PROBLEM

When it comes to your mind traveling through time, recent research points out that the future is the most dangerous culprit for stealing your thoughts away from the present moment. Psychologists and neuroscientists have only recently come to this conclusion, and rather belatedly, since for the past century, most researchers assumed that our minds were prisoners of the past. Yet, according to the American Psychological Association, as reported in the May 19, 2017, *New York Times* article "We Aren't Built to Live in the Moment," when researchers asked nearly five hundred adults during the day to record their immediate thoughts and moods, participants thought about the future *three times* more often than the past, and even those few thoughts about a past event typically involved consideration of its future implications.

Though science says you're likely to be more drawn to fixing or preventing a future disaster, this doesn't mean that the past is automatically, well, the past for you. Our beliefs are rooted in the past, and you reconnect with them at every turn. They form a comfortable and familiar story that doubles as a reason why things seem to veer offtrack. For instance, if you have a chaotic morning, you tell yourself it's not because mornings are hard for all moms but because you regularly exercise poor judgment, like the time you got drunk at your high school reunion or couldn't stop crying during a performance review. The next time you're tempted to look over your shoulder, catch your mind in the act and remind yourself that it's physically impossible to change the past, so stop wasting your limited energy going there. No amount of stewing, huffing, or puffing will *ever* change what's already occurred. It's time to move on.

With the past out of the way, let's get back to the future. I've found that the reason you spend more time focused on tomorrow instead of yesterday is because you believe you *can* impact, change, and improve it. If you walk through life looking, listening, and sniffing around for things that could go wrong, then you can work around the clock to prevent more bad things from happening in your life. It's a game of project, protect, and defend, and your dragon is running the show. I like to think of it as your dragon operating the Tilt-A-Whirl at the state fair. This machine is whipping you backward (past) and forward (future) with such velocity and force that there's no possible way you can gain enough presence of mind to see the present moment for what it is—a blessing, a non-event, and a quiet moment that follows a hard time but holds the promise for something better.

Remember, dragons thrive on chaos and uncertainty, so they cause you to project the worst even when it won't come true. Take Janna, for example, a friend of mine who learned a lot about her fearful future simply by sharing a few choice words out loud. Janna was raised in a household where stellar academics were applauded and anything less was unacceptable. Getting good grades as a child came easy to Janna, but still, she lived on edge that the bottom would fall out one day and she'd fail tenth-grade physics and be banished from her family and forced to study science via flash cards in a homeless shelter. Carrying this fear into motherhood, she also saw dark days ahead for her family, and it peaked while helping her six-year-old son with his homework. She remembers thinking one night, *Why can't he sound out the word* Ted? *Seriously,* T-E-D. *Or remember how to spell the word* and? *It's one of the most-used words! Am I pushing him too hard or not hard enough? Will he end up a derelict or with severe anxiety because I didn't guide him the right way? Wait, now he's crying. Why is he crying? He's trying to manipulate me. Or am I pushing him too hard? I'm pushing him too hard. Or maybe not hard enough! He's going to grow up to be a lazy, good-for-nothing bum who says he's writing a book but really just watches porn all day while I still do his laundry. I just know it.*

Janna and I had a good laugh over this, but after putting her inner monologue on paper, she saw how obvious it was that she was bullying and berating herself based on deep, exaggerated, and clearly unfounded fears about her future. By giving an audible voice to her worry of how she could possibly screw up her son, she could hear how painful and unnecessary it was. It was a major step for Janna in her journey to learn how to take the power away from the future and bring it back to the present. She learned to observe and pay attention to the time travel she was taking so she could be present for what was actually happening in front of her. In this case, coming up with a trick for remembering how to spell *Ted.*

WHAT ARE YOU SO AFRAID OF?

Various psychological studies have shown the average adult spends 110 minutes a day worrying, which equates to thirteen hours a week and twenty-eight days a year. That's a lot of worrying! And according to the women who attend my workshops, that number is nowhere near accurate for mothers. As one mother so eloquently said, "Who the hell only worries two hours a day? I worry at least twenty-four hours a day, if not more. If I'm not worrying, I'm worried that I don't care enough." For a mother, it's practically part of your DNA to worry, because according to the mothers in my research studies, you've never wanted to do anything so well in your life and you've only got one shot at getting it right. So, you know, don't screw it up.

All mothers worry about the health, well-being, and safety of the people we love. It's why we brace passengers in the front seat of our car with an outstretched arm, promote the energy-enhancing benefits of protein, and regularly insist our kids wear clean underwear. However, if you're a mother living with a dragon of self-doubt, your fear cuts deeper and boils down to a fear of failing. According to your dragon, things have gone wrong in the past, and if you have anything to do with it, it's only a matter of time before they derail again. So look alive, lady—the next disaster is waiting just around the corner.

Why so much fear? Well, because you know what pain feels like and you'd like to prevent it from happening again. At some point in your life, your sense of self-worth was suddenly ripped from your hands when you lost something that was yours—your lover, your A-list status in middle school, your mother's approval, your self-respect, self-esteem, or self-compassion. And even if it was thirty years ago, you know all too well that something you need and love can be taken away without notice. Worry, then, becomes a strategy to adapt to a future reality that you view as uncertain, out of control, and dangerous. You see your nervous energy as a chance to act responsibly, prevent your worst fears from coming to fruition, and motivate yourself to get your A game on.

Worrying provides the illusion of control—if you can think of all the problems with your daughter's geometry skills, you can certainly think of all the solutions. It also feels like the responsible thing to do. If your son raised his voice at his friend and you *didn't* picture him as a bully in two years, you'd be a negligent, good-for-nothing mother.

Yet in a strange twist of irony, worrying can make you feel *less* anxious, because if you're not happy with how your life is going, troubleshooting it in the future can feel like a welcomed distraction.

FEARING THE ABSOLUTE WORST

It seems strange at first that predicting the worst possible outcome for you or your family would bring you a sense of calm, but inside a dark, dragon-controlled mind, it makes all the sense in the world. When I was my weakest and my dragon was its strongest, worst-case-scenario-ing my future was a regular occurrence. I could see full-scale imaginary productions of the exact moment my career, children, parents, brother, or husband would be permanently stripped from my arms. I'm not talking about my heart racing when our home phone rang at three o'clock in the morning when something *clearly* was wrong; I'm talking about driving to the grocery store on a Sunday afternoon while contemplating which house in my neighborhood I'd have to downsize to when my husband died, since I wouldn't be able to keep up with the yard work as a single mother. I'm talking about seeing the flash go off while taking a picture of my children and fast-forwarding to that photo being blown up to poster size at their funeral. The cuter the picture, the more likely that horrific scene would appear in my mind.

This shocking form of fearing the worst is a well-documented phenomenon discussed in the 2009 internationally bestselling book *Women, Food, and God*. Author Geneen Roth describes the depth of this form of self-doubt by saying, "That's also called leaving without leaving. Dying before you die. It's as if there is a part of you that so rails against being shattered that you shatter yourself first." In my case, I was terrified that someone I loved would be taken from me and I wouldn't survive without them. So I pictured the pain frequently enough so that I'd be prepared when it hit for real—that way, I would know I could survive when they died.

It wasn't until deep into my own self-help journey that Roth's wise words illuminated the link I was creating between my loneliness in the past and my predicted aloneness in the future. The revelation shook me to my core, and I made the conscious decision that my delusional fears would no longer rob me of the amazing human beings who *were* alive and standing right in front of me. In Roth's words, I made the decision to stop trying to defy gravity.

And wouldn't you know, everyone in my family remained alive and well.

Predicting future pain is a waste of time, energy, and most importantly, the present moment. When you live for the future, you reduce what's in front of you to a mere stepping-stone to the future with no intrinsic value. If you're so focused on your child's spelling mistakes being her superhighway to prison, you're not going to notice that when you help her with her spelling homework and she improves, she smiles with pride and gratitude. That's the moment of value you are missing. Even the good things in your life become stepping-stones toward your obsession to arrive, attain, and prove your worth. The vice president title you always wanted and finally landed is one step closer to becoming a senior vice president, and the recognition you received for the fund-raising efforts is inching you closer to being seen as a good mom in the eyes of the other mothers at your child's school. Even when fast-forwarding is neutral in nature, it's still not helpful. You completely miss out on the emotional benefits of getting a massage if you're making a mental grocery list the entire time.

The key to putting an end to this stepping-stone mentality is to recognize that the present moment is all you have. It's the only thing that's real. Don't waste it by allowing your mind to live three steps ahead of your body. If you want to preserve your mental energy and save your sanity, I always remind moms to keep their mind and body in the same time zone.

IS ALL THE WORRYING WORTH IT?

Perhaps you tell yourself, as many mothers do, that all the worrying is worth it because it keeps you on your toes, pushes you to achieve great things, and prevents disasters from happening. Well, experts who study this topic don't agree. In 2015, while preparing to write *The Worry Cure*, Dr. Robert Leahy conducted multiple studies to determine whether our worries ever pay off. According to the results, 85 percent of what people worried about never happened! And within the 15 percent of events that did occur, 79 percent of the time, participants handled the difficulty better than expected and/or learned a valuable lesson along the way. This means that 97 percent of what people worry over is all rather pointless—a phenomenon that's exaggerated among dragon-fighting moms because the future they see is *more* negative and therefore *less* likely to come to fruition.

At The Mom Complex, we see this dynamic play out all the time, most notably in the work we do for companies that specialize in breakfast food of all things. Whenever we research the attitudes and behaviors around moms feeding their kids in the morning, we unearth a palpable fear of a mom worrying that her child isn't eating enough for breakfast and will end up "starving" before lunch. The fear comes up in every single study, and it is very real despite the fact that their children are unable to point to a single time when their mothers' fears were actually realized. I like to think of fear as *F*alse *E*vidence *A*ppearing *R*eal, and to this point, I always ask the moms, "I understand the concern, but has your son *ever* come home and told you he was famished and 'hangry' before lunch?" And the answer is always the same: "Well, no, but what if he *did*?" And then they shudder.

Now, it's your turn. While all your worrying somehow feels comforting, is it necessary and does it really work? In the space below, write down three examples of times you were convinced things would turn out terribly and they turned out just fine—hey, maybe even great.

Example 1: ....
....
....

Example 2: ....
....
....

Example 3: ....
....
....

It's important to realize, and expect, that what happens in the future is rarely as bad as you imagined it would be when you were freaking out about it.

While worrying about an event that won't happen might feel like a relief, science says it's anything but healthy for that poor, tired brain of yours. According to the fall 2010 issue of the *Dartmouth Undergraduate Journal of Science*, researchers discovered that your brain doesn't have the ability to distinguish between reality and hyperbole. Even when your stress and worry is hypothetical, it still triggers sensory and motor skills that affect your blood pressure, heart rate, and sweat glands. In other words, your brain doesn't know your thoughts are a *maybe*. It responds as though your worst fear is actually coming true—just like when your heart races when you have a bad dream. There's clearly nobody chasing you through the woods with a knife in their hand as you rest comfortably with a pillow between your knees in bed, but your brain believes there is, which is why it sends signals to every part of your body to freak the flip out.

When worry is induced, whether real or hypothetical, your body's response is always the same: it increases your cortisol levels, which lowers your IQ; makes you prone to heart disease, cancer, and premature aging; predicts marital problems, family dysfunction, and depression; and makes seniors more likely to develop dementia and Alzheimer's disease. Good grief. I mean, isn't life hard enough without giving yourself a heart attack or memory loss for no good reason?

GETTING COMFORTABLE WITH THE PRESENT MOMENT

Learning to live in the present can feel uncomfortable if you're not used to it. In fact, if I were a betting woman, I'd say that sitting still and being calm makes you *more* nervous than plotting and planning your disastrous future. Don't believe me? Test yourself: How long can you sit in the waiting room at the doctor's office without looking at your phone? How long can you sit on your kitchen barstool and just breathe before you grab a washrag and start cleaning up—even when there's nothing to clean up? It's okay. I bombed this test, too, when I first began tuning into my present tense. I'd challenge myself with the monumental task of sitting in a chair and taking five long, slow, deep breaths, and I rarely, if ever, made it to the third breath before jumping up because *Oh, crap! That reminds me…the plants need watering, a birthday card needs to be mailed, and I completely forgot to schedule an appointment to get my eyebrows waxed.* My inability to sit still demonstrated my belief that there was no time like the present to prevent death, destruction, and bad grooming in the future.

When you don't love (or even like) yourself, spending time alone just sitting, breathing, and recharging can feel about as comfortable as putting on a pair of wool-lined footed pajamas, zipping them up, and rolling around in them. Talk about itchy. But you *can* get used to being still and even come to love it. The more you starve your dragon from the drama and chaos it needs to survive, the more comfortable you'll be with being alone and tuning into your body and breath. And once your dragon is dead and gone, you'll crave your calm, peaceful, beautiful me time like you craved peach-flavored wine coolers on Friday nights in high school.

I'm also fully aware that it feels uncomfortable to be present because your present life is legitimately uncomfortable. A busy mind gives you something to do besides have your heart broken from watching your first-born get teased for having dyslexia, living while your sister dies, becoming a mother to your own mother, and watching your kids pack up their clothes to shuffle back and forth between your house and your ex's.

But, life is hard—and this is really the big point. You're a sensitive human being living in a messy, violent, uncomfortable, and unpredictable world. There is nothing you can do to mitigate the roller coaster that's in store for you, no matter how much you plan. You'll let your friends down, and they'll let you down right back; your children will make mistakes, and you will too. No matter how far ahead you think, how hard you push yourself to protect against what comes next, you can't change the human experience—and that experience always has and will contain a lot of pain.

Bolting from the pain you currently feel will not make it go away. Acceptance, not avoidance, is the only tactic that will ever work. Let it be okay that life is hard, and stop trying to fix what comes next. Staying where you are with what you are feeling, seeing, or sensing in front of you, no matter how hard, is the first step toward ending your obsession with worrying. Here are some tips that will help as well. I still use each of these on a weekly basis.

- **Right here. Right now.** One tactic I suggest to moms when they're feeling overwhelmed and tempted to fast-forward is to take a deep breath and repeat the mantra *right here, right now* three times—silently or out loud. This simple technique will bring you back to what's in front of you, which is life as you *know* it, not as you *fear* it.
- **Never wait again.** The very notion of *waiting* creates problems. Waiting means your body is in the present and your mind is in the future. For example, if you're waiting in the line at the DMV, you are treating the present

moment like a means to an end; you're treating it like it doesn't matter. *The Power of Now* suggests that the next time someone says to you "Sorry to have kept you waiting," you can reply, "That's all right. I wasn't waiting. I was just standing here enjoying myself: in-joy-in-my-self." What if you looked at the idea of waiting differently? What if you never waited again?

✗ **Time travel be gone.** If you catch yourself worrying about something in the future—say, not beating last year's time in the upcoming 5K—take a deep breath and say, "No more time travel." If you're able to witness your shifting perspective and the underlying emotion it creates, it will help snap you back to the reality going on right now.

BECOMING A WARRIOR

Despite all my thoughtful research, I'm not ashamed to share that the most helpful advice I've ever received came from a palm reader on the sidewalk in San Diego. A few years ago, I had my palm read by a psychic who went by the name Papa Alex. My children call my father Papa and my son's name is Alex, so when I saw his sign next to his lawn chair under a beach umbrella, I felt like the universe was trying to tell me something, and I stepped right up.

After nailing the fact that I owned my own company, had three pregnancies but only two children, and I needed to be nicer to my husband…he studied both of my hands intently, took a deep breath, and said, "You're a worrier, and you need to be a warrior."

Of course I cried.

Your worrying will get you nowhere. Just like it got me nowhere. It's time to take your dragon's power away by refusing to fan the flames with stress and anxiety over what's to come. When you release your obsession with the future, you'll help yourself greet each moment with strength, connection, wonder, and freedom. And most importantly, you'll learn to seek love from the inside and stop begging, borrowing, and stealing it from the people and circumstances around you—more on that in chapter 10. As you put these new practices into place, recognize that living in the present moment isn't just a daily decision; it's a moment-by-moment decision.

You must be open to noticing when you're creating problems out of your past and in your future, then remind your mind that you're the one who decides what you think about. No more runaway train. And when you do, you, too, will make the life-changing shift from a worrier to a warrior, and all the people you love and are trying to protect will be showered with the peace, joy, and happiness that comes from taking a deep breath, worrying less about who you're becoming, and deciding to love who you already are.

WORRYING ABOUT THE FUTURE STEALS JOY

from today.

CHAPTER 10

Looking for Love in All the Wrong Places

I'm willing to bet that you'd never doubt how much you love your children, spouse, parents, friends, household pets, or raw chocolate-chip cookie dough, but have you ever stopped to think about how much you like or dislike *yourself*? It can be a pretty uncomfortable, if not terrifying, question to consider, which is why so many of us avoid it for so long. During my dragon-fighting days, it seemed ridiculous to waste brainpower on such a seemingly crazy thought. What the flip did it matter what I thought of myself, when there were emails to send, diapers to change, and belated birthday cards to buy? The only thing I cared about was impressing others, and since positive reviews were coming in, they were my cue to keep going. As a result, any love I felt came from their approval and acceptance, instead of from me.

When you battle a dragon, unconditional self-love and acceptance are nonexistent. Your only choice then becomes working around the clock to cook, clean, race, rush, huff, and puff your way to appreciation from peers and loved ones. And maybe if you're lucky, you'll internalize a handful of their kind words and feel momentarily good about yourself. However, even when you do, your dragon is always waiting in the wings with a broom and dustpan to sweep your fleeting self-esteem under the throw rug. *Good job getting a healthy breakfast into everyone's stomachs before school,* your snarky archenemy whispers, *but there's no way you're going to pull off that new burrito recipe for dinner tonight after a busy day at work.*

Instead of shutting that bitch radio down, your heart races even faster at the idea of being underestimated, and now it's game on. You'll take its burritos and raise it a chocolate sponge cake for dessert. And just like that, a regular Tuesday evening becomes yet another opportunity to prove everyone (real or fictitious) wrong, win them over, and hope that their "wows" rain down on you like confetti in a Vegas nightclub.

All this before 9:00 a.m.

In this chapter, I'll share what it means to truly love yourself and exactly how to get there. I realize that, as goals go, this one is rather lofty, and maybe a little sappy. While it may be tough to actualize, it'll be incredibly meaningful when you do. In the end, you'll learn there's nothing sissy-ish about self-compassion—it's a proven path to becoming happier, calmer, and stronger. Healthy doses of self-esteem, confidence, and respect are critical stones in building your path to fulfillment, and they have to come from somewhere. So, when those attributes aren't alive and well inside you, you'll beg, borrow, and steal them from those around you. Keep in mind, though, that your partner, boss, neighbors, friends, colleagues, and children can't give you the kind of fulfillment you need to sustain your soul—only *you* can provide it. Attaching your self-worth to other human beings' feedback is a recipe for frustration and suffering for both the giver and receiver. And while we're talking about others, please ditch the belief that loving and caring for yourself is selfish when others need you more. The truth is, you can only give away what you have inside you to give in the first place, so the more you love and accept yourself, the more you'll love and accept others.

So, what's the deal? Do you like yourself? Are you proud of yourself? Is the love you show yourself anywhere near the unconditional love you demonstrate toward your children, or is it conditional and temporary at best, because you're only as good as your last acceptable move or your next wrong one? If the way you feel about yourself comes with any kind of clause, then it's time to send those contingency plans packing. Love is the only thing that can heal your wounds—it's oxygen for your soul, and soaking it up from what's already inside you will lead to far greater self-acceptance and calm than trying to siphon it from the outside world.

WHY BOTHER LOVING YOURSELF?

What's the big deal about whether you love yourself? You're a hard-working mother, doing her best to stay afloat. Can't you just keep your head down and get the job done without worrying about what Hallmark card you'd send yourself already? Sure you can. But if you do, your life, behavior, and actions will continue to be dominated by a dragon that runs your life with the mantra *Thanks, woman, but the next time I want your opinion, I'll give it to you.* Your dragon thrives when you put your head down, play nice, and don't ask questions. But do you?

I've learned that the first reason that loving yourself is so important is that your sense of belonging will never exceed your self-acceptance. In other words, you'll always feel like an outsider, wherever you go, because you must know your own worth to feel like you belong. This applies to whether you're trying to fit in with the parents at school, struggling to make a name for yourself at your new job, or worrying over whether you brought the right kind of chicken salad to your cousin's baby shower. It's natural to feel slightly uncomfortable in new or pressure-packed situations, but if you're operating from a deficit of self-doubt, then your general anxiousness will turn into legitimate worry that people will think you suck and tell you so, and then you'll crumble like the house of cards you believe you are.

Remember how your goal as a mom is to struggle and not suffer? Well, the superhighway to suffering in this scenario is not fully being comfortable with yourself—warts, mistakes, mishaps, and all. If you're comfortable with yourself, however, then you can take yourself anywhere and feel okay with what transpires. It's like when you think about moving, and your therapist tells you to be sure you're not just running from your problems because you take yourself with you wherever you go. In a similar way, you take yourself with you when you're among other moms and in uncomfortable situations, so it's time to love the one you're with—you.

The other reason self-love is so crucial is because how you feel about yourself influences the intentions behind your actions. When I cover this topic in my workshops, moms spill the truth like pinot grigio at a book club. They confess to volunteering for nonprofits (rather than serving on the board), not to help the underprivileged, but to appear more well-rounded to their boss; dating two guys at once not to sample the goods, but to increase their odds of finding someone who might love them; and overscheduling their kids not because their little ones love rushing from lacrosse to hip-hop on a Saturday morning, but because the mothers themselves are bored.

When you're able to improve how you feel about yourself, you won't need these ulterior motives, and as a result, your intentions will finally come from your true self and not your self-conscious self. I'm not saying that wrestling the summer sports schedule to the ground will become a joy, but doing so will no longer be the litmus test of whether you're a good person or not. Simply doing the best you can will no longer feel like failing.

WHAT NUTRIENTS ARE YOU SUCKING UP?

Of all the tasty, self-esteem-annihilating snacks you're feeding your dragon, a lack of love for yourself is central to each and every one of them. Why did I save it, then, for the end of this section? I'll tell you why: because it's also one of the most challenging to change in a calculated way. It's tricky to say that if you follow these three steps, you'll love yourself more. It's more of a visceral place at which you arrive after doing the hard work and homework to learn more about yourself and then loving the real and unvarnished person that your effort reveals. The good news is that by now (I hope) you're feeling good about the extent to which you've put your stupid dragon in its place and how much strength you've gained as a result. In fact, I'd like you to pause for a moment to really take in how far you've come since you first picked up this book. Your ever-blooming ability to adjust expectations, manage a negative inner voice, posture and compare yourself to others less, say no when you want, and remain optimistic for the future isn't just a major achievement but—wait for it—a whole lot of reason to *love who you are*.

One of the fun techniques I use to emphasize the power of self-love is to encourage moms to think of themselves as a massive tree standing in the forest. Oak, maple, cherry—you pick. The core of your being is the trunk, your behaviors and actions are the branches sprouting out into the world, and 80 percent of your growth and vitality is determined by the quality of nutrients that enter your tree beneath the ground. As you can see in the image on the next page, if your roots are deeply nourished with positive thoughts and meaningful affirmations, then the actions that branch off of you will be full, rich, and strong enough to support anyone who seeks refuge beneath their canopy (or, let's be honest, swings and jumps on them until they're about to break). Even when the winds of life try to blow you off balance, your roots will hold fast. Self-talk—such as *I'm a good human being*, *I'm worthy of love*, and *I'm doing the best I can*—is a great way to nourish and support yourself, especially when you compare it with the cheap fertilizer you usually use, such as *I suck at this* and *Even my best is never good enough*. The latter will cause your core to weaken and your branches to fracture—not to mention drape all over your feelings of inadequacy. You will not thrive, and neither will those who seek the respite and cool comfort you'd prefer to offer.

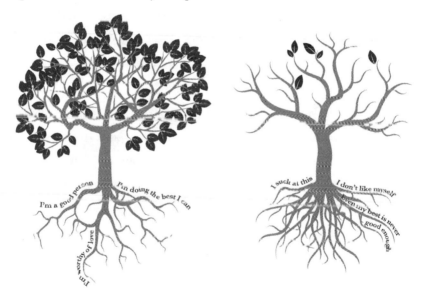

Eccentric author and academic Buckminster Fuller said that 99 percent of who we are is invisible and untouchable—meaning our thoughts, feelings, emotions, and beliefs. What's more, it's our ability to tap into these parts of ourselves and therefore transcend our physical forms that determines the quality of our lives. If you want to make sure positive vibes are pumping through your veins, get curious about the invisible parts of you. For example, the next time you look in the mirror and ridicule yourself for having a bad hair day, instead of asking yourself *Why do I always look like a train wreck?* ask yourself *Why am I being so hard on myself?*

When it comes to loving yourself, it's what goes beyond your physical form that matters.

DON'T LOOK NOW, BUT YOUR LACK IS SHOWING

The truth is, every mom could use a little extra self-love. To determine the extent to which you're feeling depleted, let's take a look at how you talk to and treat yourself both in private and public. Becoming aware of this is an eye-opening step toward changing it.

First, I'd like you to think about your language and behavior. Experts say there's a proven correlation between how you speak to yourself and how much you love yourself. So, as we talked about in chapter 5, teaching that mean voice in your head some manners will go a long way toward developing appreciation for who you are and what makes you *you*. Other aspects of self-care matter too. Are you eating poorly? Do you sleep fewer than six hours each night? Have you forgotten your girlfriends' names? And when was the last time you went to the gym, got a massage, or walked around a mall alone? It's been a minute, right?

I know a mom who once treated herself to a nutritionist when she struggled to fit healthy eating habits into her busy lifestyle. During the first meeting, she inquired about tips for limiting the "time-consuming" vegetable prep because she didn't have time to wash and chop them.

The expert's response? "If you don't have time to *slice a cucumber* for yourself, we really need to work on your self-love." Life is a balancing act, and if the scales are tipped in everyone else's favor but yours, it's a sign that you don't value yourself enough to take care of yourself.

Another key indicator of how you feel about yourself is the company you keep. Think about the characters in your life, past and present. Do you continue working for a patronizing boss who points out everything you do wrong and nothing you do right? Are you dating or married to someone who sweet-talks the dog more than you? Do you make out with boys with *PLAYER* on their license plate? (Okay, that last one was for my former self.) If so, it means your dragon has you convinced that you and whoever is bringing you down are a match made in heaven because you'll never find anyone better to put up with your shortcomings.

One of the greatest payoffs for loving and respecting yourself is that you'll become astutely aware of those who aren't supporting you in a way you deserve. When you love and respect yourself, you will rather quickly hit your quota for tolerating others' bad behavior. And you won't have to look far to find the people who are blocking you from seeing and appreciating your own bright light. The Negative Nellies in your life don't hide who they are and might as well be wearing T-shirts that say *Get ready, lady. I'm going to walk all over you.* You can blame them all you want, but at the end of the day, you're choosing to participate. You keep showing up for exactly what you know is coming. People can't walk all over you unless you lie down and let them.

Case in point: My friend Sydney's self-love took a beating for eighteen years as her verbally abusive husband and father to her children yelled, screamed, and berated everyone in the house into believing they were always wrong, and he was always right. The brave decision to file for divorce and walk away from her dream of having the ideal family followed Sydney's *even braver* realization that she and her children deserved to be valued, loved, and respected. And by removing the biggest naysayer in their lives, it opened a plethora of pathways to self-love in the form of immense pride, respect, and strength. Once the darkness in their lives was gone, they could finally see and appreciate their own value.

What's keeping you from embracing your greatness? In the space below, list a few ways in which you're cutting yourself off from the rich nutrients of self-love. Be honest about the negative actions (yelling at yourself, eating terribly, staying in an unhealthy relationship) as well as the absence of positive actions (going to the gym, giving yourself a break, recognizing your own strengths) that affect multiple areas of your life.

WHAT I'M DOING:

WHAT I'M ALLOWING OTHERS TO DO:

What did you learn? Remember what the whale watcher taught us back in chapter 3: what you know, you love, and what you love, you protect. If your examples depict a mother who doesn't protect her time, talents, and sanity, then you need to keep working on the self-love. The more supportive, caring, and compassionate you are toward yourself, the more you'll do whatever it takes to protect all the things that have the potential to make you happy.

FOR ONE, STOP SEEKING EXTERNAL APPROVAL

I find that how much of a boost you need from others directly correlates to how little love you give yourself. This deficit can show up in a number of ways. Maybe you hang around your boss's desk, hoping to put another "great job" feather in your cap, or if you're like me, cuddling with your kids while point-blank asking them what makes you a good mom (why be subtle?). There's nothing wrong with seeking a pat on the back every now and then—we all need to fill our tanks, and doing it all alone can feel, well, incredibly lonely. But while it's okay to *want* people to like, respect, and value you, it's not okay to *need* it. You have to be able to navigate life without being addicted to the adrenaline drip of other people affirming your awesomeness.

Growing up, I was so unable to operate without these affirmations that I literally built a shrine to my accolades in my bedroom. I covered every inch of a gigantic bulletin board next to my bed with my bartered self-esteem. If any poster, report card, or birthday card said something nice about me, I put it on the wall: *I'm proud of you* from my father, *You're doing a great job* from my mother, *I love you* from my brother, *What a star*

204 SLAY LIKE A MOTHER

you are from my grandmother, *You're a special human being* from my aunt. The fate of my self-worth rested in the hands of those I loved, and I was convinced that if I memorized their sentiments, then I'd finally believe them myself.

If only it were that easy.

I realize now that my enormous wall of fame made me feel very blessed. I was loved by incredible people, but it did little to help me love myself. In other words, I looked at their notes *about me* and thought it said a lot *about them*. Why the switcheroo? Because no matter how frequently other people shower you with affection, their sentiments fall on deaf ears and blind eyes until you first learn to love yourself. And where's the proof of that? In my parents' attic, where I found myself twenty-five years later reading the *same* notes through very *different* eyes. With my dragon dead and gone, I poured through six shoe boxes of love notes, and I found myself agreeing with each and every one for the first time. *Good point, Mom, Right on, Brother*, and even *I know, right? That was kind of me to cut my grandmother's grass.* It's amazing how your view of external validation changes when you learn to love yourself. You no longer search for it like water during a drought, and when you do receive it, it simply feels like a thoughtful acknowledgment of what you already know to be true.

Therefore, an excellent litmus test for evaluating your self-love is how well you can take a compliment. Right now, when you hear what you've been dying to hear—that you're super smart, a real style icon, beyond hilarious, and a great mother—let me guess what happens: you toss the observation back like a hot potato. You dismiss your stellar outfit by saying it was on sale; you shut down your ability to squeeze in grocery shopping between birthday party pickups by saying, "You should see me on a bad day!"; or if someone congratulates you on your promotion, you tell them you were simply "in the right place at the right time." Sometimes, being on the receiving end of a compliment makes you so uncomfortable that you just deflect one right back: "Oh, wow, aren't you nice?"

This isn't because you're modest, but because you don't find truth in these glowing words. Your opinion about yourself trumps how other people feel about you. In this case, your own negative beliefs are blocking true and genuine outside love from getting in. That's the way this love business works. Your opinion of yourself is the one that matters and the one you need to focus on moving forward. I've met far too many women who have all the external approval one could ever want yet remain lost and longing for more. Lawyers who say they're not smart enough, millionaires who swear they're not rich enough, mission workers who aren't giving enough, stay-at-home mothers who aren't mom enough. It's entirely possible to fill your life with accomplishments and still feel empty, to have incredible gifts and never see them, to receive glowing compliments and not believe them. That's because what's really missing isn't the intellect, money, generosity, or dexterity to be better. It's an inability to see your own strengths.

WHEN RELYING ON OTHERS LETS YOU DOWN

Receiving external approval and not believing it is one thing, but what happens when you don't receive it as often as you'd like? If you're only able to accept yourself to the degree that you feel accepted by others, then when you don't feel the love, it launches you into a self-doubt-induced tailspin that you fully believe in earnest. For example, if the room mother at your daughter's school gives you a little side-eye, you're obviously a big, fat loser, and if your father questions why you didn't make it to church last Sunday, you're clearly going to hell. Basing your self-worth on what you're worth to other people is a *very* volatile, unpredictable, and exhausting way to live. It's like constant emotional whiplash. And it's not sustainable. As behavioral scientist and bestselling author Dr. Steve Maraboli often says, "If you fuel your journey on the opinions of others, you are going to run out of gas."

What's worse, allowing others to solely fuel your self-worth allows your expectations (here we go again…) about other people's love to become too high. Nobody can ever seem to give you the love you need, then you tell yourself that it's because you're unlovable. You get pissed when your husband doesn't say your new haircut looks fabulous, your brother doesn't say you're a hero for taking care of your sick mother, or your children don't say thank you for making and raising them. But the truth is, your loved ones can't give you a sense of pride in who you are, an appreciation for how far you've come, or a mere acceptance of the life you lead—at least not in any consistent or substantial way. In fact, according to research from The Mom Complex, they can't even thank you on a regular basis. No joke: a mother is thanked, on average, once every twenty days—so please stop holding your breath.

Suzanne Hanky, a parenting coach and family educator with over thirty years of experience and five children of her own, says she sees a lot of wounded women in her office who are looking for others in their life, particularly their children, to validate their worthiness. The true danger, as Hanky describes it, is that if your emotional need for affirmation is not being met, you can unknowingly expect your child to fill in the gaps. And when they don't, you feel *even more* rejected. Anger, sadness, and feelings of incompetency show up over routine events such as a child refusing to clean their room, no longer wanting to hold your hand in public, or making an ugly face at the homemade lasagna they used to love. Then, according to Hanky, a child can easily internalize your overreaction as the fact that the love they *are* giving you doesn't make you happy enough. My favorite advice from Hanky, which I use regularly, is that it's your job to make yourself happy, not your child's.

BLAME IT ON THE SHAME?

So many of the roadblocks to loving ourselves come from our past, whether that's related to when your dragon was born or simply moments you regret and that make you worry that you're a bad parent or person. If the idea of loving yourself for who you are, *as you are*, feels about as comfortable as sleeping on a bed of tacks, then you've likely crossed the line from feeling guilty about your decisions to feeling shameful about who you are as a human. According to Brené Brown, critically acclaimed researcher, bestselling author, and fellow mother, the difference between guilt and shame can be summarized as *I did something bad* versus *I am bad*.

Let's say you had to skip out on your son's school play on Friday because your boss called a last-minute meeting. If you feel guilty, you're able to limit the blame to the *behavior* you exhibited. The voice in your head might say something like *I hate that I couldn't be at the play to see his debut performance as a peach tree.* Shame, on the other hand, knows no bounds and quickly becomes a painful personal indictment: *I'm a horrible mother for putting my job before my child.* According to Brown, shame enters the equation for so many mothers because not only do we feel afraid, out of control, and incapable of managing our demanding lives, but our anxiety is also eventually made unbearable by our belief that if we *were* smarter, stronger, or better, we'd be able to handle everything life throws at us.

When you make a mistake as a mother or think about the mistakes you've made in the past, on which side of the guilt/shame equation do your most intimate thoughts and feelings fall, and how does this relate to self-love? If you're like most mothers I work with, the answer is shame, but you refer to it as guilt. The word *guilt* has become so synonymous with motherhood, with flippant labels like *mommy guilt* plastered all over the internet, that we've become blind to the self-sabotage of shame that's silently lurking behind the scenes and eating us alive.

Every year, I spend thousands of hours interviewing mothers and, oh, how I *wish* their greatest challenge was guilt. What a gift that would be to feel mildly annoyed with the tough choices they have to make every day. Some days, I feel like launching a public service announcement directed toward mothers that declares *Bring on the guilt! What a relief it would be from all this shame.* The different outcomes between the emotions are dramatic. Guilt leads to corrective measures and the belief that you'll do better next time. Shame leads to self-loathing and the belief that you never have been and never will be good enough.

CONDITIONAL VERSUS UNCONDITIONAL LOVE

When it comes to loving your children, they might be cute—but, man, they sure can do a lot wrong. Remember how they refused to clean up after themselves as toddlers? Or that time they mistook your house for a party boat when they were in college and you were out of town? And while these knucklehead moves make you crazy in the heat of the moment, you still love them with every ounce of your being. They can do a lot wrong and nothing wrong at the same time. This, of course, is how unconditional love works. The code of conduct for unconditional love doesn't say *Thou shalt do no wrong*. It says *I expect that you can and will make mistakes, and I will love you anyway*. It's the *anyway* that means everything.

Yet you don't afford yourself the same luxury! Because you've felt the wrath of conditional love from yourself and others somewhere in your past, it taught you that love is a conditional game, wholly dependent on accomplishing X, Y, and Z. In this black-and-white world, mishaps are not allowed, and mistakes are strictly forbidden. We live in fear of our next wrong move, and when it inevitably happens, we cut ourselves off from the one thing that will get us through the hard times—knowing that it's okay to make mistakes and that we're worthy of another try.

According to my research, one of the major turning points for shifting your love for yourself from conditional to unconditional is your ability to accept the full picture of life: that the experience you're having will always come with highs and lows, good times and bad, positive decisions and poor choices. Instead of seeing your mistakes as worthy of a tongue lashing, inner peace comes when you view them simply as part of the human experience. If you need a physical reminder of this, you could do what many mothers tell me they do: wear a Lokai bracelet. This popular bracelet, inspired by the mindfulness movement, is made with a series of clear beads anchored by one black and one white bead. The black bead is filled with a grain of sand from the Black Sea, which is the lowest point on earth and meant to remind you to remain hopeful when you're feeling low. The white bead is filled with a drop of water from Mount Everest, which is the highest point on earth and meant to encourage you to remain modest when you're feeling high. There's nothing quite like a physical reminder—a bracelet, a necklace, or even a tattoo—to remind you that the goal isn't to do *no* wrong but to have a little perspective when you do. The energy we give off when we achieve this balance can only come from love.

I encourage you to start practicing the art of unconditional love—complete with no ifs, ands, or buts. At no point in this process do I want you to question *why* you're worth loving more. You don't have to lose ten pounds first or help your child learn his ABCs in Mandarin. Just as you are, you are 100 percent worthy of love. This is enough. You are enough. And self-love can be unlimited if you allow it.

Here are a few exercises that can put you in the right frame of mind and heart for seeing and appreciating the greatness that's already inside you.

* **You go, girl.** List three positive things that happened yesterday and what your role within each one of them was. These don't have to be life-changing events. Let's say your son picked up his puzzle pieces without you asking, which means you've taught him how to politely clean up after himself, or that your friend agreed to go for coffee, which means she enjoys your company. It's so much easier to love yourself when you're able to see the good in you, both with and without others' endorsement.

✱ **Take a compliment.** The next time someone pays you a compliment, I want you to bite your tongue. Don't interrupt their monologue, don't clench your cheeks and wish it would hurry up and end, don't change the subject, and most importantly, don't say anything other than "thank you." *Period.* Your silence will help you hear what they're saying, and your lack of rebuttal will help you actually believe it. I normally reject the idea that practice makes perfect because perfection is rarely a positive goal, but in this case, I think being perfect at taking a compliment is extremely healthy!

✱ **Love songs.** The next time you're stuck in traffic or in the carpool line, find a classic love song station on the radio and turn up the volume. Close your eyes and resist the temptation to imagine your long-lost boyfriend or ex-husband singing it to you, and imagine you singing it to yourself. Imagine that it was written by you and for you. Suddenly, Van Morrison's line "I've been searching for someone exactly like you" reminds you the importance of self-love, Alison Krauss's lyric "You say it best when you say nothing at all" reminds you to keep your negative inner voice quiet, and Disney's "Let It Go" from *Frozen* no longer exists to entertain your daughter but to enlighten you.

TAPPING INTO WHAT'S ALREADY THERE

Once you start putting these practices into place and get a taste of the joyful, warm, and liberating high that you can't buy and that comes with loving yourself, it's hard to turn your back on this endless resource again. You'll realize your capacity to love yourself never really left—you didn't lose it, squander it away, or loan it to someone else. You were just hustling to feel loved for so long that you couldn't see your own love waiting in the wings to save you. Self-love is an unlimited resource at your disposal twenty-four hours a day should you choose to tap into what it can do for you. What will you become when you love yourself? I went from a follower to a leader, from exhausted to deeply fulfilled, and from a lover of fried chicken tenders to raving fan of tofu.

If I have anything to do with your future, the first thing you will become is a dragon slayer. The previous seven chapters have been about cutting off your dragon's food source in order to loosen its power over your life, decisions, and actions. You've traveled a tremendous distance—gaining insight, perspective, and willpower along the way. Now with you at your strongest and your dragon at its weakest, it's time to take out your sword and put an end to all the fighting, fretting, and self-doubt forever.

Get ready, dragon—we're coming for you.

FIGHTING TO
FEEL LOVED
by others
BLINDS YOU TO
THE LOVE THAT'S
ALREADY
within you.

PART III

GETTING RID OF YOUR DRAGON

for Good

CHAPTER 11

Three Secret Weapons for Killing Your Dragon

*I*f you can successfully reduce the amount of time you spend on the self-defeating practices I discussed in part 2, you can remove your dragon's hold over you and begin to operate from a more genuine and emotionally satisfying place. But by no means does this mean your dragon is dead—a little hungry maybe, but still patiently holding out for its next meal and not out of the picture yet. Up to this point, we've focused on negative behaviors that need to be eliminated because they feed your dragon: yelling at yourself when you get passed up for a promotion, assuming your child will never learn any manners, and constantly comparing yourself to the room mother at school. In this chapter, however, we'll turn an important corner—away from negative reactive behaviors and toward positive and proactive measures that will instill a deep sense of inner peace and contentment.

Over the years, I've seen three tools prove to be the most effective weapons when a woman is ready to slay her dragon. Dead, gone, finito, see ya sucker. Your artillery of choice? It's not the aggressive slings and arrows you may expect to use because you've been wielding them on yourself all this time. I'm talking about gratitude, self-compassion, and honesty. Or, as a mother in one of my workshops summarized, "I appreciate my fortunes, forgive my mishaps, and willingly share the highs and lows of my life without fail."

In part 3 of this book, I'll walk you through the steps it takes to nail these attributes and celebrate who you truly are. Gratitude means deploying mood-enhancing gratefulness for the reality that's sitting in front of you; self-compassion involves being warm and understanding with yourself when you're imperfect; and honesty entails getting real with yourself and others about the life you live and not the one you're posturing to maintain. That's right: you're going to demolish your dragon with the newfound goodness you've worked so hard to see and embrace in yourself.

I know it might feel good to use some good old-fashioned violence, anger, or brute force on your dragon—to let out years of frustration in one single, gory bloodbath—but the only way to slay the beast within is to kill it with kindness toward yourself and your truth. Why? Because positive personal change will never come from flinging vitriol, because love conquers hate, and because paying tribute to your already magnificent soul is guaranteed to put out your dragon's fire for good. Practicing gratitude, self-compassion, and honesty will become your guidepost for taking a different path forward in life—one riddled with much less confusion and friction than you face now. It reminds me of when singer, songwriter, and author Portia Nelson summarized her life in a piece titled "Autobiography in Five Short Chapters."

Chapter One of My Life: I walk down the street. There's a deep hole in the sidewalk. I fall in. I am lost. I am helpless. It isn't my fault. It takes forever to find a way out.

Chapter Two: I walk down the same street. There's a deep hole in the sidewalk. I pretend I don't see it. I fall in again. I can't believe I'm in the same place! But it isn't my fault. And it still takes a long time to get out.

Chapter Three: I walk down the same street. There's a deep hole in the sidewalk. I see it there. I still fall in. It's a habit! My eyes are open. I know where I am. It's my fault. I get out immediately.

Chapter Four: I walk down the same street. There's a deep hole in the sidewalk. I walk around it.

Chapter Five: I walk down a different street.

Your new path won't always be lined with daisies; perfection is rarely a healthy life goal—not for you, not for anyone. But when you stop seeing yourself as a hopeless, wandering victim and get past your pity party with a dead dragon slung over your shoulder, your journey simply won't be guided by fear anymore. You'll be called to make decisions for you and your family that are driven by what leads to more gratitude, not more hustling; what will cut you a break, not give you a hard time; and what feels true to you, not what impresses others. And the day you become aware that you're walking down another street, *by choice*, I promise you'll exhale the heavy fear and burden you've been carrying around for so long.

WHERE'S ALL THIS OOMPH GOING TO COME FROM?

Believe it or not, you already have an arsenal of gratitude, self-compassion, and honesty within you. These characteristics innately live in our pure and perfect souls that were modeled upon creation after a universe or God that is pure and perfect as well. These are not new skills to be learned but values you already teach your children and use on others. It's time to summon these resources for yourself.

I also have confidence in your ability to gather them up because dragon-fighting moms have a big, fat secret I alluded to earlier, and this is incredibly important. Though we've been acting like we don't believe we are worthy of love, time, inner calm, or sanity, deep down, we have felt we deserved it. We knew it existed for us because we've fleetingly experienced it—once in a while, we'll catch a glimpse of ourselves in the mirror or see how our kids look at us and feel the proof that we *are* good enough. Even still, we've chosen to slump down into what's comfortable—self-flagellation, dragons, *blah blah*. It's easier to look for confirmation that you're not worthy (dwelling on how your mother-in-law scoffs when your daughter runs outside without a coat) than acknowledge the quiet testament that you are (your son says he "loves you times infinity"). It's like when you slow the car to stare at a wreck on the side of the road but drive right past a field of flowers. We constantly look for the disaster, not the beauty. Everyone tends toward a negativity bias, but the inclination is strongest for those of us who are drawn to chaos and drama, especially when it's what we perceive happening within ourselves. I want you, instead, to gravitate toward what makes you feel good, because there is, as I hope you've learned so far, so much goodness within you. These words might make you shiver a little, but you must continue to choose to like what you see when you look in the mirror. You must continue to realign with the pure and perfect soul you were born with and that you're worthy of.

THIS ONE IS ON YOU

When you make the decision to slay your dragon, you choose to stop complaining about what's holding you back and start making your own way. One of my all-time favorite spiritual masters and religious teachers—Sri Swami Satchidananda, founder of a world-renowned ashram dedicated to world peace in Buckingham, Virginia, not far from my home—knows the power of taking matters into your own hands. I almost fell out of my chair when I once heard him say, "Stop getting so angry at the roaches for being in your kitchen when you're the one leaving the crumbs on the floor and inviting them in." What a remarkable truth! Only you can stop feeding your dragon the crumbs of your self-esteem. You are the only one who experiences the pain, destruction, and suffering that this behavior has left in its wake, and this means you are the only one who can continue changing your course in the specific ways you need.

The other reason this fight is your responsibility to win—and also why I would like you to take a kinder, gentler approach in combat—is that while your dragon's roar has been triggered by forces outside yourself, it lives within you. This is to say that your dragon *is* you. Granted, your dragon is a fictitious and distorted view of reality that *you* created and *you* kneel down and honor every day, one that represents your greatest worries gone wild. And it's not a part of you that you like. But it isn't separate from you, and unlike a schizophrenic who robs a convenience store and blames it on another personality, you need to own that your dragon isn't separate from who you've been until now. So, while we must slay, we must also preserve *you* in the process. This is why you absolutely must decide to use your three weapons with all your might and commit. I don't want you to *try* it; I want you to *do* it. If you do not resolve to finish the job, you will continue to feel unloved and unappreciated, and your fears will only gain more steam. And just in case any part of you is thinking that all this mom stuff will go away on its own when the kids are older and leave the nest or when you lose ten pounds or…or…you know by now that's not the truth. The beast inside you will just refocus its efforts on a new area of your life.

GRATITUDE: BEING THANKFUL FOR WHAT'S WITHIN AND AROUND YOU

The first fatal blow is dealt when you express gratitude toward your dragon by thanking it for the role it has played in your life. Yes, I just said that—and I mean it. If my own dragon hadn't beaten me down so badly, I wouldn't have gained the strength to end its life and begin mine all over again. It taught me that putting my happiness in the hands of other people is a mistake and that I get to decide how to spend my time today, tomorrow, and every day after. So just because your dragon made you feel like crap for years on end doesn't mean you have to stoop to its level when you're about to say goodbye. Besides, you know that you can't fight fire with fire; you have to dump water on it, right? Expressing gratitude is an ideal way to cool down and reduce the intensity of this destructive situation. I also believe that everything happens for a reason, and while your instinct might be to assume your dragon was in your life to destroy it, maybe it was there to teach you a thing or two—to shine a light on areas that warranted growth.

The thing is, gratitude in general fills us with peace and content-ment. It's worth practicing as you ramp up to kill your dragon and long after it's gone. Now, I don't know about you, but I usually find gratitude exercises a little silly—better for a woman who has endless time to sit cross-legged in lululemon capris on a silent Kripalu retreat, not a mom like me who can feel more scrambled than a plate of eggs. Besides, how are you supposed to feel grateful for frenetic days that include cleaning a lot of dog accidents and telling your child to stop throwing Matchbox cars in the toilet? Well, there are ways—the annoyances that stick out in our heads aren't the *only* part of our days. I'm sure you've heard self-help experts suggest keeping a gratitude journal and jotting down anything that comes up that you're grateful for. I find myself *saying* I'll do these things but never delivering. So, here are two ideas I think you might like better.

First, try turning gratitude into a game with your children. As part of our bedtime ritual, I lie next to each one of my kids and we name our peak and pit from the day, i.e., the best and worst part of the past twelve hours. It's super easy and doesn't require a lot of brainpower or time (that alone is something to be thankful for). Of course, I'm grateful for whatever brings my kids joy but find myself equally if not more grateful when learning about the parts of their day that sucked—for example, when my son was teased at school for mispronouncing words, my daughter beat herself up for not getting a perfect score on her math test, and (gulp) how I yelled at them for misbehaving. These insights tell me that nobody in my house has it all figured out and that we're okay talking about our imperfections. It's clear that we still love each other just as much, if not more, when we fall short. And even when my kids' pits involve me, I don't let myself get too down about it; I just try to breathe through it and learn from what I hear. It's also less stressful to hear about my kids' challenges, and for them to share them, when we're lying in the dark, cuddling with stuffed animals. It helps me listen and respond with compassion and kindness.

Another gratitude practice I like is putting pen to paper and making a list. (Do not let your mind wander and turn this into a to-do list... *I see you...*) I used this approach a few years ago after our family took our first cruise together, and I found myself incredibly overwhelmed by the number of people on the ship, the fact that I felt trapped, and how I couldn't stop throwing up from seasickness no matter how much anti-nausea medicine I ate, drank, or stuck to my body. As the trip came to a close, I had a bad taste in my mouth (probably from so much barf), and I desperately wanted to be grateful, not bitter, for the experience. It wasn't a perfect holiday, but we still managed to log lots of memories! So on the final day, my daughter and I made a list of the fifty amazing things we saw or experienced on the cruise, which included eating soft-serve ice cream five times a day, getting henna tattoos, contorting our bodies to fit in the tiniest shower on the planet, and reenacting that famous scene from *Titanic* on the front of the ship. It was a fun exercise, and it forced me to recognize that it was a better vacation than my mind was allowing me to remember.

All these practices help me breathe easier, relax more, and see the inherent good that's easy to overlook when you're ordinarily zooming around. What I love most, though, about gratitude is that it can't coexist with resentment, fear, and anxiety. Try it—try to be thankful for a sunny day but simultaneously pissed off that it will rain tomorrow. Your mind finds it impossible to process both emotions at once because they're in direct opposition to each other.

So if you had to express gratitude for what your dragon has taught you, what would you say? Consider the following example from a mother in one of my workshops, and then come up with your own.

Dear Dragon:

Thank you for suffocating my self-worth for so long, because when I finally reclaimed my love, respect, and admiration for who I am as a human being, it all came flooding back stronger, brighter, and better than ever before. Living in the deficit of my self-doubt taught me that I will never, ever live that way again. I've never been more sure of anything in my life. And I have you to thank for it.

Love and hugs,
Allison

Dear Dragon:

....

....

....

....

....

....

....

....

....

SELF-COMPASSION: FINDING THE GOOD

Once you're able to see and appreciate both the good *and* bad, the highs *and* the lows that your dragon has brought into your life, you can turn a little self-compassion your way. Don't assume that being kind to yourself is a negative or self-serving thing to do—there's nothing self-pitying, indulgent, or self-centered about this. In fact, it's that very mindset that prompted Kristin Neff, PhD, associate professor in human development at the University of Texas, to write the 2011 book *Self-Compassion: The Proven Power of Being Kind to Yourself.* In it, Neff shares how women tend to have quantifiably lower levels of self-compassion than men, even while we tend to be more caring, empathetic, and giving toward others. In other words, we think, *Of course other people struggle; it's a fact of life, and I want to be there to help. But it's not acceptable for me to struggle.*

Why does this happen? According to Neff, self-compassion involves putting three components into action: being kind and caring toward yourself rather than harshly self-critical, framing imperfection in terms of the shared human experience, and seeing things clearly without ignoring or exaggerating problems. This isn't an easy trifecta for anyone, much less a dragon hoarder, to achieve. And remember the exercise you completed in chapter 5 where you outlined what you would say to a friend who made a mistake or was going through a tough time versus what you'd say to yourself? Chances are, you realized it was important to be kind and not critical of your friend, that we all make mistakes, and that it was clear to you that she should move on. Yet to Neff's point, these are harder conclusions to arrive at when you're talking about yourself.

So how can you talk a friend off the ledge when they feel like a failure, yet fall short when trying to do the same for yourself? Because you believe that your own mishaps are ten times worse than any human who ever lived. But remember, that is simply a belief you created and backed up with validations. It was never a reality. When I was in high school, I was *convinced* I was a horrible person because I lied to my parents about my whereabouts on a Friday night. Therefore, when their wrath of disappointment rained down, I couldn't dismiss it like my older brother did. I saw it as proof of what I'd come to believe about myself, and it glommed onto any prior self-doubt I had. It also blocked me from accessing any form of self-compassion.

COMPASSION IN ACTION

Need a little boost to launch your self-compassion? The next time you forget to pack your son's lunch or get schooled by your office manager for jamming up the printer again, take a deep breath and repeat the mantra *I am so much more than this situation.* You can even be more specific to the situation and role you're meant to play in each. For instance, it's okay if you don't make it to every school function, because you're more than a mom; it's not the end of the world if the office manager gets upset with you, because you're so much more than an employee. No matter what situation you're in and no matter where the criticism is coming from, there's always more to you than the current circumstance that's bringing you down. You're greater than the sum of your parts, your life is more meaningful than your highs and lows, and sometimes you have to step outside your daily tasks to remember that you're a human *being*, not a human *doing*.

As women who wear far too many hats in a day, we put so much energy into our different roles that it's not uncommon to see each one as *extremely* important and therefore narrow the focus of your time and effort to the one duty in front of you and worry that if you make a mistake, it makes you a bad person.

Give the exercise above a try when the going gets tough, and if you're brave, you can try it on for size when things *go right* in your life as well. When you get your next promotion or win the cookie-selling competition for the Girl Scouts, and you're tempted to do a little dance and wrap your identity around your newfound success, remind yourself: *I'm so much more than this situation.* Getting too high with the highs can make the times you fall short feel like an even bigger letdown and overall divide. Just keep in mind that you're not a robot; you're a human with lots on your plate, and the more compassion you extend toward who you are versus what you accomplish, the happier you'll be.

And before you know it, your self-compassion will transform who you are in a big way. When the mishaps of your past no longer feel like mistakes but life lessons, you'll see them as valuable learning experiences for the future. You'll also find that failure feels less scary, and you'll become more likely to take risks, such as starting your own company or signing up for an aqua Zumba class when you have no rhythm. And finally, when a tough situation threatens to steamroll your Monday, you'll be more resilient and ready to deal with the fallout. We're all equal in the universe's eyes, and we're called to be as compassionate to ourselves as we are to each other. Making sure you give yourself enough of the love and support you're giving others will do wonders for cutting off your dragon's oxygen supply. With all that love and support flowing around, there will be less negativity for it to inhale and blow back in your face.

HONESTY: SPEAKING YOUR TRUTH EVEN WHEN IT'S HARD

Your next step is opening up additional aspects of yourself that you've been hiding from others. In chapter 6, we talked about speaking your truth in a big, bold coming out, but here, I'm suggesting you simply be more of who you are on a regular basis—and that you weave this into what you do every day. In your truth, there is no more room for lies.

Your goal here is to live honestly and in alignment—meaning, how you feel on the inside should match how you present yourself to the world. I'll never forget when I became acutely aware of this need for myself—at the chiropractor's office of all places. I've suffered from lower back pain for as long as I can remember, and it was triggered at every turn: as a competitive gymnast as a child, carrying cranky kids around as an adult, and regularly stuffing myself into uncomfortable airplane seats as a professional. Several years ago, while having my back examined, when the doctor swiveled her computer screen around to show me the scan of my spine, which was out of alignment in multiple locations, I burst into tears. (Shocking, I know.) The scan perfectly illustrated my life at the time—polished on the outside but completely misaligned and in pain on the inside. By pretending nothing was wrong and avoiding asking for help from experts, I had made my back worse until my only treatment option was regular trips to the chiropractor to get my spine back in line, plus months of physical therapy to keep it there.

It wasn't lost on me that if I'd been honest with myself earlier on, I could have saved myself years of pain and escaped the expense and inconvenience of so much therapy. Staring at what living my life out of alignment had physically done to me, I vowed to avoid the same mental fate. Before I got dressed, I made a pact to open myself up to the world, X-ray style. If I was going through a hard time, I would talk about it; if I was grumpy, frustrated, or overwhelmed, I would admit it and ask for help. No more cover-up, double life, and secret shenanigans—I wanted no place for my dragon to hide. Of course, I was worried my broken bits would be rejected, but I knew that continuing to hide them would cause more long-term pain.

My hope is that you don't have to break down in a doctor's office to give yourself permission to live honestly. Perhaps your experience will be more like my friend Marti's, whose extensive efforts to make it seem that she had it all were most obvious on Facebook. Though she was regularly exhausted from working, arguing with her boyfriend, and worrying about her daughter, you'd never know it from her profile, jammed with perfect photos and adorable puppy pics. One night while Marti was stuck on the airport runway during a delayed international business flight, she passed the time by scrolling through her Facebook timeline—and as she tells it, "I nearly had an out-of-body experience" because she realized how amazing she managed to make herself look on social media and how grossly it didn't match what was really going on. So, she posted this:

I think Facebook is one of those places where your life tends to look pretty perfect with all the posed pictures, fun times, great memories. Sometimes, when I look back at my feed I see only positive, happy things. While I would say I am genuinely at a good place in my life, what I've chosen to post put an extremely positive filter on it. So, just for the record, here's my attempt to round out my Facebook story all at once. (1) All that travel all over the world is awesome AND it is also thoroughly exhausting and lonely at times. (2) My amazing job doing interesting things is really an end result of me spending five years struggling and ultimately failing at a startup I co-founded where I also lost almost every close friend I had. (3) My beautiful, smart, amazing daughter is a product of divorced parents when she was 2, followed by 15 years of endless work to make sure that living in two houses with two totally different families is never more of a burden than it should be—since I am responsible for it. (4) The truly happy relationship with an amazing boyfriend of almost 12 years…to say the first 8 were the hardest is an understatement. I am not even sure people knew how we made it. (5) The amazingly cute dog farts and they really stink (otherwise she is actually close to perfect). These are my truths, and I'm sticking to them.

Not only did Marti get honest with herself and her friends in a public way that made it hard to take back her truth, but she also inspired other moms to do the same. By the time she'd landed in Singapore, Marti had dozens of emails, comments, and text messages from other moms saying they admired her honesty and were going to follow suit.

LONG-TERM SURVIVAL TECHNIQUES

Once you get in the regular habit of practicing gratitude, self-compassion, and honesty, I swear your doubts and insecurities will melt into thin air and smoke like the wicked witch at the end of *The Wizard of Oz*. It won't happen overnight, but it *will* happen. As you go, there are two expectations you can set now. First, it seems to take most moms I work with about six to eight months before their dragon is significantly gone from most areas of their lives (it's been around for a long time, so it's not going to disappear overnight). Know you'll take three steps forward, maybe one back, then six more in the right direction. Next, while we're not fighting violence with violence, know that it's perfectly okay and even recommended to let your frustrations out in a way that works for you. Taking back control of your life, decisions, and actions is hard work, and you'll undoubtedly need an outlet for exhaling. Maybe you'll be like the moms who take physical exercise to the next level to get it all out or even like one mother I know who once shared that when she found herself tempted to feed her dragon during this final phase of slaying, she'd go in the guest room and beat the you-know-what out of the pillows while saying, "I *will* take back control of my life!" It's a fantastic technique, if you ask me.

The final expectation I'd like you to put in place is that even once your dragon is dead and gone, know that you'll still encounter bumps in the road, a.k.a. triggers, that send your mind reeling like it always has. The difference is that this time, you'll have the right tools to recognize that what's confronting you is *not* your dragon but a shadow of your previous fears, and you'll be able to move past the flashback fairly quickly. En route, keep an eye out for people and events that trigger the fight-or-flight reaction you know well. You can simply stop yourself by becoming aware that it's happening before things go too far. This helps you correct the habit in real time.

For instance, when I was asked to serve as the Richmond Christmas Mother, a well-known tradition in my hometown where a prominent mother leads an effort to raise over a quarter of a million dollars to support underprivileged families during the holidays, I was triggered pretty quickly. I started out not feeling worthy of the appointment, which sent me into a tailspin of setting the overly ambitious goal of *doubling* the previous year's goal and raising more money than any of the eighty-nine mothers who came before me. Old habits die hard, I guess.

A few weeks into the season, I could sense, however, that my intentions were misplaced. The clue was when I noticed that my language wasn't aligned with my truth: when family and friends would say how amazing the appointment was, I told *them* I was proud, but I told *myself* I was terrified of failing and worried that the organizers would one day realize they shouldn't have picked me for this job. As soon as I caught myself, I dropped the inner story line that I wasn't good enough, erased the ambitious fund-raising goal from the equation, and got on with my merry Christmas way of helping as many families as I could. If it sounds simple enough, that's because it was. The minute I sensed that my old tendencies were sneaking back, I shut them down. And with all that pressure off my chest, I had the time of my life in the role of a lifetime.

LET FREEDOM RING

Should you encounter triggers that set you off the way the Richmond Christmas Mother post did me, you may need a bonus weapon in your back pocket and that is to accept that your self-doubt has been more than a little addicting. Sounds crazy, right? When you think of addiction, you might think of heroin, porn, and old ladies playing the slots in Vegas, but the definition of *any* addiction is the compulsive engagement in rewarding stimuli, despite adverse consequences. Sounds more familiar now, right? And though feeling beaten down by self-doubt hardly seems like a reward, it has been your primary form of motivation for years. Your relentless self-criticism, condescending comments, and forecasts for failure have pushed you to do better. But it hasn't worked out for you because addictions don't work out for anyone. The false sense of pleasure you derive in the moment invariably turns to long-term pain, so you keep going back for more pleasure with the hope that it will dull your pain until, eventually, you no longer feel you can stop. But you do have choices—and choices are freedom. They are your way out of this cycle. So woman up, because you've already chosen to stop, and there will always be bumps in the road. But you will overcome them. Look how far you've come already!

During my workshops, I used to go on about how unhappy I was for the twenty years I lived with a dragon inside me. That is, until my husband indicated he was tempted to take that perspective personally, since he played a significant role in my life for fifteen of those years. This forced me to think harder about what I meant when I said I was unhappy, and the more I considered it, the more I realized the hole inside me wasn't a lack of happiness, but a lack of freedom. I felt trapped, caged, chained to a hamster wheel going nowhere. But now, with my dragon dead, I'm free. Free from feeling stuck, from hustling to be loved, from a heaviness I couldn't put my finger on, and from presenting myself as anyone other than exactly who I am.

You deserve this kind of freedom—every human being does—and once you get out of your own way, it's yours forever. It's your birth-right to bring yourself more laughter, less suffering, and more deeply gratifying breaths. I'm talking about a freedom that's so fulfilling and contagious that you'll inspire others to chase their own liberation as well. America's anthem, "The Star-Spangled Banner," ends with what a blessing it is to live in the "land of the free and home of the brave." It's a wonderful reminder that you will never be free unless you are willing to be brave. Standing up for your own inner freedom is a *very* brave and worthwhile thing to do.

LET NOTHING STAND IN THE WAY OF *standing up for yourself.*

CHAPTER 12

How to Listen to Yourself Once You're Free

*T*hough your dragon is officially dead and its sanity-crushing behavior has just about left the building, you may still hear echoes of it in your memory from time to time—and that's perfectly normal. What's great is that you finally know not to trust it, and what I'd like you to do now is focus on a more reassuring whisper that's been trying so hard to emerge. When you get rid of fear, something really incredible happens—you allow a more positive inner voice to surface and slowly guide you in all you do. Some call this your highest self, intuition, or even God. It doesn't matter what you name this voice; what matters is that you know how to recognize it and listen.

A TALE OF TWO VOICES

You might be a little freaked out over whether you'll be able to tell the difference between your dragon's echo, which has the ability to take you down in a heartbeat, and your wise inner voice that's been buried for too long but has the ability to lead you to the promised land of inner peace. I can practically hear you fretting *What if I think I'm following the good one and it's really the bad one? What if a third voice moves in and I lose my mind?* These are valid questions.

Good thing the two voices have nothing in common, which makes them simple to tell apart once you know the rules of the road. The echo of your dragon sounds, well, just like your dragon when it was alive—aggressive, loud, exasperated, suspicious, condescending, and cruel. Your intuition, however, sounds calm, cool, and collected, doesn't come from a place of fear, and wants to see you succeed. It is quiet, still, sounds affirming and supportive, and exists to bring out the best in you. It also likes to show up in a flash as a hunch or aha moment. Follow *this* voice's direction, and life will unfold in a way that feels authentic, protected, and intentional. Here's a quick snapshot that I often share with mothers to illuminate the difference.

YOUR INTUITION   YOUR DRAGON'S ECHO

YOUR INTUITION	YOUR DRAGON'S ECHO
☐ Quiet	☐ Annoyingly loud
☐ Compassionate	☐ Cruel
☐ Supportive	☐ Paranoid
☐ Comes from your gut	☐ Comes from your ego
☐ Wise	☐ Fearful
☐ Quick	☐ Obsessive

Your intuition always has the highest good in mind, for you and the world at large. In fact, remember how you felt during those rare, small glimpses in the mirror when you'd think *Good job, Mama* after helping your daughter nail a math test or *You've got this* before walking into the new parent meeting at school when you knew no one? That was your intuition talking. But it's critical to also understand that this force in your life is not *always* positive. Your inner voice is also meant to keep you out of trouble, push you into uncomfortable opportunities that promote growth, and help you learn from mistakes. If you can recall a time when you apologized for phoning in a project at work or missing your friend's birthday, your intuition is what caught you in the act, reminded you that you could do better, and pushed you to do the right thing. This is to say, you can't assume that your intuition is always full of compliments, but it does have your best interest in mind, which includes calling you out to help you and others grow. The difference is that unlike your dragon's echo, the reminder feels kind or neutral (unless the situation is dire, in which case your inner voice will jolt you like thunder, and that's good too).

In addition to using different tones, these two voices lead you down very different paths. As you've surely experienced, following your dragon's fighting words rarely leads to contentment, but as you'll soon see, hanging on your inner wisdom's words will direct you down a path of deeply meaningful and fulfilling experiences. Your intuition knows you better than you know yourself, and the more faithful you are to it, the more energized you'll be. It's a direct line to your happy place, and you simply cannot afford to remain deaf to your intuition's message.

Keep in mind that you can only *listen* to a good vibe when you're paying attention to what it's saying. Your intuition speaks in a whisper, much like a wise monk sitting in the corner of a garden, waiting for his turn to speak. It's as if he hasn't been able to get in a word edgewise because of the irrational and aggressive dragon in another corner that's been screaming, stomping its feet, and demanding your attention for so long. What's amazing is that your intuition has stood by you all along, trying to interject yet never turning away when you wouldn't listen. As bestselling author and life coach extraordinaire Martha Beck likes to say, "If you're waiting for wisdom to outscream paranoia, get comfortable. It's gonna be a long wait." Wisdom is far stronger than fear, but while fear gladly forces itself on you, wisdom will do nothing of the kind. Wisdom comes from the soul—it's the language of a protective and larger universe—and you must quiet your mind to hear your soul and this larger force speak.

A NEW KIND OF BODY LANGUAGE

One way to start tuning into your intuition is to become aware of how your body responds to different scenarios. It's a technique that Beck describes in her 2001 book *Finding Your Own North Star* called *body compass work*. She says the most fascinating thing about your intuition is that you don't have to teach it anything. It is always paying attention, is pointed toward your highest good, and knows exactly what amps up your energy and what depletes it. It's like having a GoPro camera attached to your head and a lie detector strapped to your chest at all times.

The best way to tune into your body and instinct is to read your own body language. Interpreting these cues isn't a new skill; you've been honing it for years. It's how you know your son hates your new eyeglasses and your daughter has a crush on a boy in her class. No words are necessary to communicate these messages, because their body language is loud and clear. Now it's time to turn this master skill inward and start translating your own body language. For example, when you're waffling between a yes or no decision, close your eyes, picture each scenario in full color, and notice how your body physically reacts. For instance, if you imagine yourself volunteering for the

Easter parade at school, do you feel your stomach clench into knots, or do you smile at all the toddlers in furry suits? When you think about leading a fund-raising event at church, does your throat constrict and your skin itch, or do your shoulders relax and make you feel expansive and alive?

Let's give this a try. Close your eyes and imagine yourself having another child. How does your body respond to your hypothetical new life? If you're like most mothers, you either go all buttery in the knees and take a big old virtual whiff of baby powder, or your chest constricts, you forget to inhale, and your armpits start sweating. You must know and trust that your body and intuition sense what's best for you, and you must be willing to listen—not with your mind but with the *feelings* that these scenarios create when you consider them.

Some of the most compelling proof of how your body communicates intuitive wisdom has been discovered by Antonio Damasio, a neuroscientist and professor at the University of Southern California. In a 1996 study known as "Iowa Gambling Task," Damasio and his team conducted an experiment in which subjects could choose between decks of cards to win money. The choices included two good decks that turned up consistent profits and two others with riskier cards. While it took about fifty cards for subjects to decide to switch decks and eighty cards for them to explain why, the subjects' skin was simultaneously monitored for signs of stress. After drawing just ten risky cards, the skin tests showed that all the subjects' bodies were displaying signs of anxiety. Yet nobody spoke a word! Our bodies have the amazing ability to fire signals faster than rational thought, and according to this study, left to our rational minds, we'd wait five times longer to get out of a risky situation.

Why does your body register instinct and feeling faster than your mind does? Well, for one, there are one hundred million neurons in your gut assigned to processing external stimuli and sending signals to your brain, which then translates them to help you make your next choice and action. However, this process doesn't happen right away—your mind will edit, censure, and resist some of the data, especially if emotions are triggered. So, if you want to tap into the truest part of you to make decisions, you might as well go to the source and skip all the *mishegas*—start in the gut.

I got a lot of practice with this when I launched my own company. Once I knew I wanted to leave my advertising job and be an entrepreneur, I didn't decide on my ultimate business plan by attending conferences, reading business books, or reviewing dozens of case studies. Instead, I begged other entrepreneurs I admired to have lunch with me and then let my body respond to what they said. When my friend Allison explained the benefits of taking on outside investors, my stomach clenched so tightly that I lost my appetite and knew it wasn't the right path for me. When an acquaintance named Natalie discussed quarterly meetings with her board of directors, I became parched, mustered one of those awkward dry-mouth gulps, and vowed to avoid that structure at all costs. Yet when a friend of a friend named Karen talked about the control and freedom that came with feeling beholden to nobody but her own bottom line, my heart fluttered and felt determined to take the leap. Looking back now, I can see what a fascinating turn of events it was for me in the self-confidence department. I didn't ask other entrepreneurs how I should set up *my* company; I asked them how they set up *theirs* and then I let my intuition guide me toward the solutions that would bring me the most happiness and fulfillment.

Can you tell the difference between how you feel when you hear your dragon's voice or echo and when you sense your intuition? Fill in the blanks below about a time you listened to each and how your body responded to the information it heard.

My dragon's voice/echo once convinced me to ....

....

....

How I felt after: ....

....

....

My intuition convinced me to ....

....

....

How I felt after: ....

....

....

ACTING ON YOUR INTUITION

While it's essential to pay attention to your intuition, what you feel means nothing unless you act on it. Chart a new course and step out of your comfort zone. Be brave enough to do what your instincts know is right before your brain gets caught up in the details and potential downsides. My general rule of thumb is that if the vibes you get from your body compass are positive, then you must at least explore the possibilities. If they're mixed or you're unsure, take a pass or do some more homework before you make a decision. And if the vibes are negative, have the courage to say no.

My friend Maritza McClendon, a doting mother of two and the first African American to make the U.S. Olympic swim team and medal, has a remarkable story about how she first slayed her dragon and then followed her intuition to a deeper truth. McClendon grew up as a promising athlete with an intense and overbearing father. He was a former professional athlete whose career was cut short due to injury, and his need for her to excel took its toll over the years. As she recalls:

My father put me down when I didn't win a race, telling me it was my fault and that I should be embarrassed for letting my team down. During the 2000 Olympic trials when I didn't make the team but still had the opportunity to compete in other races, he handed me a plane ticket and told me to go home. He said if I couldn't be the best, there was no use competing for anything else.

Because of her father's hurtful words, McClendon lived with an all-consuming dragon of self-doubt from ages thirteen through nineteen that left her feeling alone, empty, worthless, and contemplating suicide. This was how she felt on the inside, even though she smiled for cameras, proudly shook hands with fans, and happily signed autographs. It wasn't until years later that her therapist helped her realize that she swam for herself, not for her father, and it was time to stop feeding her dragon. She went on to achieve her goal of competing in the 2004 Summer Olympics, setting records for her country and breaking racial barriers along the way.

During her first post-Olympic speech, however, McClendon addressed five thousand high school students with her father's, and dragon's, echoes in her head. She had come so far, yet she still worried that she would embarrass her father or lose the public's interest if she didn't glamorize her success story and tell people what they wanted to hear. So, during this first speech, she kept to an original script that painted her story as happier than it was. Once offstage, she heard a quiet voice inside her say, *Tell the truth next time. You deserve it, and so do they. Free yourself and these young swimmers at the same time.* She listened to her instincts and, instead of drafting any speech ever again, spoke spontaneously from her heart during talks. She talks openly now about the pressure she felt and how she managed to cope with repeated disappointments.

And now that McClendon is a mom, she finds that her gentle inner voice guides her all the time. For instance, when her husband's grandmother suggests her kids are suffering because she "always" travels for work, she trusts her intuition, not relatives, to decide exactly how much time away from home is too much. McClendon also relies on her compassionate inner voice to stop her from coming down too hard on her children for reciting their ABCs too slowly or not finishing all the food on their plates—much like her dad would with her. Today, she works hard to show compassion and support to her children much like her mother always did.

JUST SAY OM

Meditation offers a great environment for listening to and following your inner voice. The practice is nothing new (it's ancient, in fact) but its popularity has exploded in the past few years and is now being incorporated into school curriculums, university training programs, and professional sports. Why? Because it does so much good. Legendary basketball coach Phil Jackson credits many of his Chicago Bulls national championships to teaching Michael Jordan and the rest of his team about meditation. It's even woven into our U.S. military training. We now offer soldiers *mindfulness-based mind fitness training* to guard against post-traumatic stress disorder. It makes me chuckle when meditation experts such as Lodro Rinzler, chief spiritual officer of MNDFL, a NYC-based meditation studio, point out, "All of the sudden, people are saying meditation can help you, but Buddhists have been saying, yes, we've known this for 2,600 years."

During my own self-help journey, I didn't know a thing about the practice until author Gabrielle Bernstein introduced me to the concept in her 2011 bestselling book, *Spirit Junkie*. I was hesitant to try it at first—meditation seemed designed for older men wearing robes in a monastery, not a young mom worried about what toys the kids were going to shove up their nose. But in an effort to find calm amid the chaos, I was willing to try anything. The first time I meditated, I didn't pull out a fancy cushion or incense. I simply sat in silence in my entrance foyer at 11:00 p.m. after everyone had gone to bed. As Bernstein instructed, I kept my first meditation time very simple. I took a lot of deep breaths, more than I had in years, and I silently repeated a version of the mantra Bernstein had suggested: *I welcome guidance. I am willing to see the truth. What will you have me do?*

I lost track of time, but it didn't take long for my heart and soul to respond. Halfway through my first sitting, tears like I had never experienced ran down my face. I wasn't sure what was happening, but I was certain I wasn't crying. I took a deep breath, curious about this new liquid on my face, and I realized they were not tears at all. They were a sign that my soul was thawing out—my dragon was gone, and I could breathe again. I had closed off and frozen the inside of myself twenty years ago, and it had remained that way ever since.

On a Tuesday just before midnight, in my foyer, I began breaking open. When I got quiet and stopped talking, stopped pretending, and *really* started listening to what was going on inside me, it warmed my soul. As I sat in silence and invited guidance into my life, my intuition showed up in spades when a soft-spoken voice, that sounded exactly like my own voice, said, *Well done. You're done.* Done with the fear. Done with the anxiety. Done with the denial. Done with living my life for other people. Someone once told me that meditation is the most extraordinarily ordinary thing you can do, and my trial run did not disappoint. When I got still and listened to my truest self, lo and behold, my soul had something profound to say.

I was hooked from my first go at this practice, but I get that there's a chance that it won't, or hasn't, felt so extraordinary to you. That's fine! The goal isn't to have a life-changing experience right out of the gate; it's to tame what the Buddha referred to as your "monkey mind"—a noggin filled with drunk monkeys jumping around screeching, chattering, and carrying on endlessly—as a means to end your suffering. If you're just getting started, I'd like to address a few of the more common roadblocks I hear and how to move past each.

✱ **I don't have a special spot for meditation; I just have a messy house.** When it comes to where it goes down, nothing fancy is needed. I will confess that after I fell in love with the practice, in an attempt to make it feel more official, I immediately went out and splurged on a beautiful white meditation mat and cushion. Then after using it only three times, my cat marked her territory by peeing on it, and I had to throw it away. It wasn't the end of the world, because sitting upright with no lumbar support hurt my back, so now I just choose to lie down. Yes, that's allowed. So my current ritual consists of lying on my back in my home office with one small couch pillow under my head and another one under my knees. This is first thing in the morning before anyone wakes up and starts freaking out about burnt toast, backpacks, and almost missing the bus.

✱ **I don't know how to do it.** If sitting alone in silence for ten to fifteen minutes makes you want to throw up, bring a teacher along for the ride. If you go without any guidance the first time, you'll probably focus on making your grocery list, wondering what to wear to work, and then beating yourself up for not being able to maintain mental silence. During my maiden voyage, I repeated several mantras to ponder from Bernstein and it worked like a charm. You can also download a popular meditation app and be guided by a teacher or expert. This format reduces the itchiness of being alone with your thoughts and teaches you valuable breathing techniques, mantras, and philosophies to use all day.

✳ **My mind keeps wandering.** It's okay. That's what minds do. During meditation, the goal isn't to forcefully shut your thoughts down. While sitting in silence, your job is to recognize thoughts as they come up, calmly release them, and bring your attention back to the most centering force you have inside: your breath. *That* is the superpower muscle you're training: the ability to see thoughts from the past and future popping up and calmly let them pass without hitching a ride to another time zone that's filled with anger, anxiety, suffering, or frustration. One visual exercise that's been helpful to me is picturing myself standing on the side of the road and imagining that each one of the thoughts that pops into my mind is sitting in the back of a pickup truck that's driving down the road in front of me. My job isn't to put up a roadblock and prevent the truck carrying the *I can't believe my cat ruined my fifty-dollar meditation cushion* thought from entering my psyche. It's to *let it* enter and then let it pass by without getting in the truck with it. If you do this frequently enough, your mind will no longer be your worst enemy; it will be your best friend, because it's calmly able to identify and dismiss the mental distractions that used to take you down dead-end roads.

✳ **Who has time for this kind of thing?** I get it—no mother needs another task on her to-do list. But you only need to set aside ten to fifteen minutes out of the 1,440 we have each day. And if that feels too hard to pull off, you may have to (eek) consider that you might not want inner peace as much as you think you do. I suggest siphoning time from superfluous activities, such as scrolling through Instagram for the eighteenth time in one day or listening to guided meditations through headphones while commuting to work or waiting for a flight to take off. There's no rule that says meditation has to be done at home or even first thing in the morning. Grab any ten minutes you have and go for it.

As you can see, meditation doesn't require a lot of pomp and circumstance, take a lot of time (thank goodness), or rely on much training. But because it's simple doesn't mean it's easy. Meditation is a bit like putting on liquid cyeliner: at first, it's hard, messy, and you're all over the place, but with practice, it looks and feels natural. For me, meditation has been nothing short of life-changing. By giving in and trusting the process even when it feels like I'm watching paint dry, I've become *very* clear about what energizes and depletes me. I follow my instincts, not the crowd, and I can usually make major decisions about my future, career, and family in a nanosecond because I know who I am and where I want to go. The more you engage your instinct, the easier it is to trust and use it at every turn.

HOW MEDITATION LEADS TO MINDFULNESS

To be honest, I've always found the term *mindfulness* a bit contradictory. I think it should be called *empty-mindedness*, because the goal of living in the present moment is to avoid being distracted by irrational, fear-based thoughts. Perhaps you're familiar with the kind of empty-mindedness that occurs when you've checked off your entire to-do list (all fifty-six things) and then breathe a gargantuan sigh of relief, kick back in your chair, and find respite in the fact that your mind is *finally* clear from all the crap you were suffering over. It feels like crossing the finish line at a marathon or scoring a home run for the corporate kickball team. But we all know the high of that empty-mindedness feeling only lasts about thirty-six seconds before you start thinking of other shit you need to put on your list. As I tell the mothers in my workshops, inner peace doesn't come from having a clean mind when you have a clean slate, but from having a clean mind in the midst of a very *full* plate.

In my experience, meditation is one of the best ways to train your mind to embrace mindfulness when you need it the most. A lot of moms think that sitting in silence and focusing on your breath is simply about finding calm in *that* meditative moment, but it's so much more. Meditation is referred to as a *practice* for a reason. If you can practice the art of not being a slave to your irrational thoughts during calm and quiet moments, then you can bring the practice into play when you *really* need it in your day-to-day life as a parent, professional, spouse, what have you. In other words, what you practice in meditation sticks with you for the long haul.

For instance, let's say one morning you listen to a guided meditation that invites you to think of your truest self or your soul as the deepest part of the ocean—always stoic, always calm—and to imagine the circumstances of your life as the winds that rough up and blow around the water on the surface. While you digested this during a moment of silence, this metaphor will come in handy later in the day when your daughter freaks out about her science test. Instead of riding with her on the waves of anxiety, you can draw strength from the stability of your core and be the calm in the storm that she's looking for you to be. And when you and your husband get into a fight, you're better equipped to know that this, too, shall pass and that a small argument doesn't have to send your mind fast-forwarding to an imaginary, fatal divorce. When you're in meditation, you groom and practice what it means to be still so that in real time, you can be. In a way, meditation is like Kegel exercises for your brain.

I CAN SEE CLEARLY NOW

In the midst of parenting hullabaloo, it's hard to see clearly enough to make good decisions when your thoughts and fears are giving you emotional whiplash. When I catch myself inundated with worrisome thoughts about the future, I lean on a technique I learned through a guided meditation. The goal is to separate from your emotions, one emotion at a time, and simply recognize them rather than react to them. So when you ask your daughter five times to clean her closet and find that after she says she's done, it still looks like the backroom sales rack at Bloomingdale's, don't think, *I'm so angry right now!* Instead, you'll simply note, *Oh, look, there's anger.* After all, you are not anger; anger is an emotion. Watch it come, then watch it go. Every time I feel a new negative emotion coming on, I witness it instead of becoming it.

The result? When I was nervous about a meeting I had in New York City, I thought, *Oh, look, there's anxiety,* and the anxiety decreased; when I came across my grandmother's number in my cell phone and realized I couldn't call her because she'd recently passed away, I thought, *Oh, look, there's sadness,* and the sadness dissipated; and when my children were screaming at each other before dinner, I thought, *Oh, look, there's frustra-tion*, and the frustration decreased. It even works on positive emotions by magnifying them. As I watched my partner at The Mom Complex nail a new business presentation, I thought, *Look, there's pride*—and wouldn't you know, the pride *increased*. When you become aware of your feelings like this, it leaves room for your instincts to quickly direct your body to respond to what you're experiencing with whatever your best interest is at the time, whether that's to move on from the moment or amplify it.

One of the greatest benefits of living and parenting mindfully is the ability to think clearly and make decisions based on what is true to you rather than muddled distractions from your dragon's echoes or Negative Nellies around you. Think of your mind and decision-making ability as a mason jar filled with water, muddy sand, and rocks. The more you shake the jar, the murkier and foggier the water becomes, right? But if you can calm your mind, sit in the stillness, and avoid rattling the jar around, then the mud and rocks settle, and the water becomes quite clear. And *that* is the environment and mindset in which you want to be making decisions.

When you can see the world in front of you as it actually is, you prevent your fears from muddying your decisions. My dragon once blinded me from seeing that my emotions, fears, and insecurities were running my life, but not anymore. Nobody is in charge of my life, choices, and decisions other than me. Being able to see that has invited ample concentration and clarity into my life. As you've started paying attention to and distancing yourself from your irrational thoughts and fears, what have you noticed? How has the calmness, clarity, and concentration affected your life? It's about to affect others' lives too.

Inner peace ISN'T THE ABSENCE OF STRUGGLE, BUT THE ABILITY TO *deal with it.*

PART IV

IT'S

Bigger

THAN YOU

CHAPTER 13

The Ripple Effect of Triumph

*O*nce you're free from daily self-doubt, you'll notice two main things. First, parenting will still be hard, but frankly, you'll find the struggle to be a huge relief. Second, you'll begin to see the power you have to make different choices for yourself. Options that you previously hadn't accepted as options for *you* will begin to open up. You'll realize you have a choice whether to attend or skip the school fund-raiser; drive your son to soccer practice or ask another family member to do it; bake cupcakes from scratch for a school birthday party or do a drive-by at the grocery store. You won't worry whether you look like a bad human or bad mother. You will do what you need to do to keep going, and you'll see that it doesn't have to be the torture you once chose to participate in. You'll also see that while dragons are mean and ferocious, it takes two to battle.

In this chapter, I'll share the many positive ripple effects that come from releasing your self-doubt and following that all-knowing intuition of yours. For instance, you'll regularly see the good in who you are and the decisions you're making, those decisions will become faster and easier to make, and you'll yell at your family a lot less for the choices they make. You'll feel lighter as you step into acceptance and learn to let things go. In fact, buckle up, because you'll inspire yourself just as often as you inspire others. Isn't that what you wanted all along?

What I love so much about watching moms go from self-doubters to dragon slayers is noticing how they dramatically affect the people around them. I'll never forget a woman I met at one of my workshops named Nancy, a seventy-two-year-old mother who, as a child, rarely felt worthy. Her parents had trouble dealing with a series of hardships, so she never learned how to face them for herself in a healthy way. As a result, it was easy to criticize herself and pretend to be someone she wasn't. Nancy suffered with her self-doubt until she finally came into her own in her late fifties, and she never turned back. What's amazing is that even though her kids were out of the house at that point, she still feels she's a better mom and has helped her daughter be a better mother, and together they encourage Nancy's grandchildren to share and celebrate every aspect of who they are. Nancy's ripple effect cut across generations in her family, and the women now understand what it is to move forward from a place of strength. You, too, have the power to make such an impact; you have the ability to pay your new perspective forward.

INTRODUCING THE NEW YOU

One of the first places where many women feel the positive ripple effect of slaying their dragon is in the effortless creation and maintenance of a healthier lifestyle. When I was in the throes of performing, pleasing, and perfecting, my annual physicals always came attached to the same warning signs from my doctor. Each year, he explained, "Katherine, despite the fact that you appear healthy on the outside, your body is far from healthy on the inside. Your stress level, complete lack of exercise, and affinity for fried chicken tenders are having adverse effects on your health. Your cholesterol is high, you've had gestational diabetes with both pregnancies, and your ratio of fat to muscle mass is in the range of someone who is, technically speaking, obese." I heard his advice but never heeded it for two simple reasons. First, while I might have been rotting on the inside, I had the metabolism to hide it. In other words, I appeared healthy on the outside, so how bad could it really be? Second, my accomplishments at work were *very* important to me, so any time spent chopping, cooking, and stirring food or prancing around a gym in biker shorts would have taken time away from advancing my career and therefore my self-esteem. Translation: it wasn't going to happen.

Any effort I exhibited to join a gym, sign up for a new workout class, or order a side salad instead of french fries lasted about six days before I threw in the towel and got back to my tried-and-true excuse that my intense schedule simply made it impossible for me to even *think about* working out or eating better. So, how did I eventually find the time to take care of myself? I stole it from maintaining my fake self and gave it to my real self. Instead of staying up until midnight to perfect a research report, I started going to bed early so that getting up for meditation didn't feel like a pain in the butt. Rather than working through lunch and devouring a bag of barbecue potato chips, I made a routine of getting out of the office and attending lunchtime yoga classes. And when it no longer felt necessary to make my mark in every meeting at work, I became open-minded about attending events at my kids' school that previously felt like a big, fat interference in my life. There are only twenty-four hours in a day, and as you'll soon see, when you stop wasting your time making yourself look better, you can use that time to make yourself feel better.

The transformation was swift and remarkable. This former lover of frozen pizza started cooking brussels sprouts on the outdoor grill, the girl who had scoffed at *any* form of physical exercise was standing on her head in yoga class, and the mother who used to cherish lounging around like a sloth on Sunday nights found herself spending that time attending a meditation group at a local Buddhist sangha. I was eating better, sleeping better, and my skin even looked better—so much so that friends often inquired about my secret weapon. They'd ask, "Wow, your skin looks so great. What are you using?" My response was always the same: "Happiness. I highly recommend it."

Though I wasn't putting anything new on my skin, I was taking care of myself in a new way and putting something new inside my mind, most notably that I was a worthy, lovable, and really good person. I started treating myself to the time, respect, and attention that I deserved, and I realized that making changes wasn't as hard as I feared it would be. I found myself naturally making choices that made it easier to take care of myself, such as selecting a location for my new office that was within walking distance to both a popular yoga studio and health-food store and within biking distance to my home for those days when I needed to clear my head and get some fresh air. Having a healthy lifestyle within arm's reach reduced my tendency to try and bypass it. There was no shame in my healthy game.

Many of my closest friends and family found it baffling that I was able to find more me time than ever while in the throes of starting my own company, but the secret was that slaying my dragon made me a happier and more fulfilled person. That made me want to be a healthier person. In fact, I've come to believe that being happy leads to being healthy, not the other way around. I've seen the same in mothers around the world. I get emails and letters all the time with stories of heroic women explaining that they thought they had poor eating or exercise habits because of a lack of time, only to realize that it was actually a lack of self-respect. And once they kicked their dragon to the curb, they lit up from the inside and wanted to protect that light. They were no longer an afterthought in their own lives and could maintain their newfound inner peace, calm, and happiness above all.

SQUEEZE OUT THE GOOD STUFF

Your own health and happiness won't be the only beneficiaries of your dragon-free life; those around you will feel the love as well. When you stop picking battles with yourself, you pick fewer fights with your kids; when you love yourself more, you love those around you more; and when you don't judge yourself, you're able to accept others more freely. I've always loved how bestselling author and spiritual guru Dr. Wayne Dyer introduces this phenomenon in his 1997 book *Manifest Your Destiny* by asking an incredibly obvious yet profound question: "When you squeeze an orange, what comes out?" Everyone with a pulse knows the answer is orange juice and that no matter how hard you squeeze, grapefruit juice will never fill your glass. The same is true for your life.

Just like it's unimaginable for grapefruit juice to spill from an orange, it's impossible for peace and joy to pour from your soul when you're filled with dread, self-doubt, and fear. The emotions inside you often end up on the outside, so don't think for a second that seeking and maintaining peace, happiness, and inner calm is somehow a selfish act. It's not. It's also true that no matter what you use to squeeze an orange—a fancy juicer, your own two hands, or a sledgehammer—the same thing emerges every time. According to Dr. Dyer, we believe our anger and frustration come from other people's doing, but the truth is our response to any given situation has little to do with who is squeezing us and everything to do with what's already inside. For example, your son's refusal to turn off the TV last night didn't make you angry. You had anger inside you long before SpongeBob juiced it out of you. After slaying your dragon, there will be much more love and acceptance flowing both inside and around you than in the past.

My friend Lisa, a devoted mother to six kids and eight grandkids and who attended one of my workshops, has seen firsthand the positive ripple effect of slaying her self-doubt. Lisa's dragon was born when she was a young girl. Throughout grade school, it was constantly pointed out to her that she was the youngest child in her class. While she held her own academically, Lisa could never quite shake the fear that she'd fall behind or that she needed to work harder than the other kids just to keep up. This steady drumbeat of fear sat passively beneath her accomplishments throughout her life until it multiplied into a furious, fire-breathing dragon in her forties when Lisa was tapped to become the CEO of the family business— a multimillion-dollar manufacturing company that produces two million frozen twin pops every twenty-four hours (that's a lot of twin pops!).

This appointment, which would send most men pounding their chests with pride, had the opposite effect on Lisa because she suffered from what's known as impostor syndrome, the inability to internalize her own accomplishments and a persistent fear of being exposed as a fraud. Despite evidence of the sufferers' competency, psychologists say impostor syndrome is most common in high-achieving women for whom success is dismissed as luck, timing, or as a result of deceiving others into thinking they are more intelligent and competent than they believe themselves to be.

After reading several of my blog posts about the importance of standing in your own greatness, Lisa began to seek insight, comfort, and wisdom from other successful women—specifically how other female CEOs came to believe they were worthy of such awesome recognition and responsibility. Today, Lisa would tell you that the greatest catalyst for slaying her dragon was her desire to take a compliment and pay forward the pride and joy she felt from it. As she describes it, "I wanted to believe those who said I was a great leader, boss, or mother and not rain on that parade with my own negative thoughts. I learned to listen to those who love me and believe what they believe about me." What I adore most about Lisa's story is the effect that her gratitude and confidence have had on her family. Her daughter Jennie says that watching her mother's evolution taught her that confidence comes from within and that it's incredibly contagious. Holly, a woman who works for Lisa, once told me that watching Lisa's strength and confidence increase over the years inspired her to embrace who she is, not what others think she should be. And Lisa's loving husband even pointed out that Lisa's belief in herself has helped her put faith in others' innate goodness and strength. In fact, she recently implemented a new program at work that helps former prisoners find work within her company.

Lisa is not alone in her journey to finding happiness and having the effects of her success inspire others to do the same. According to a fascinating research study titled "Dynamic Spread of Happiness in a Large Social Network," published in the *British Medical Journal* in 2008,

"Everyday interactions we have with other people are definitely contagious, especially in terms of happiness." To study the spread of emotion, researchers plotted the emotional health and social connections of five thousand individuals over nineteen years. The results showed that when a person is happy, the people around them become happy as well. Friends living nearby experienced a 25 percent higher chance of feeling happy themselves, and next-door neighbors experienced a 34 percent increase in happiness.

What's more, researchers found that each additional happy friend increases your probability of being happy by about 9 percent, while a five-thousand-dollar increase in income increases your probability of being happy by only about 2 percent! So, not only is happiness contagious, but it's also an incredibly powerful force for good—more so than cash money. What's really cool is that the ripple effect of happiness wasn't limited to those who came in contact with the research participants. It spread across three degrees of separation, reaching friends of friends and even strangers.

KNOWING WHAT YOU WANT

As you gain strength over your own choices, decisions, and life, it's important to start using the effects of your internal and external transformation to achieve what you really want out of life. Several years ago, my life coach helped me identify how I really wanted to spend my time, energy, and efforts. After one of our sessions, she asked me to write down my definition of success in life and then do the same for how I defined success at work.

I'm not afraid to admit that I stared at the blank page of that first assignment for a *very* long time because I had never once thought about what it meant to be successful at anything other than my career. I thought long and hard before writing the following:

> *Success is about being happy. It's about breathing deeply and knowing that my family, my experiences, and my life are well lived. It's about dropping everything and visiting my grandparents, taking time to send loved ones handwritten notes, watching my kids giggle, sitting on the front porch at the river with my parents, and walking down the street holding my husband's hand. But most importantly, success means having the presence of mind in each of these moments to recognize that I already have everything that matters in life. It's taking a deep breath, looking around, and feeling full.*

I wrote from the heart, not overthinking anything. Once I finished, I was astonished at how *obtainable* success was! Heck, I was already experiencing it on a daily basis, and obtaining still more would not be particularly challenging. It would actually be quite easy. What a relief! Next, I moved on to my definition of success at work by writing:

> *Success is making the lives of mothers easier. It's doing for other mothers what I've done for myself—helping find inner peace and alleviating the doubt they carry around every day. Success also means creating a work environment that allows women to use our power and passion to do good by aligning our lives with a worthy cause. Success is ensuring that every-thing we do is meaningful and moving.*

Immediately after putting my pen down, I noticed that my definition of professional success no longer had anything to do with external approval and everything to do with using my strength and influence to create a positive impact. Wow. What a difference life without a dragon makes.

Teasing out my personal and professional paths made me realize that when it came to success, I was both right and wrong my entire life—right to be driven by it but wrong to blindly follow everyone's definition of it. By taking the time to draft my own blueprint, I had a new guide as I made daily, if not hourly, decisions about how to spend my time. Take a minute to draft your own definition of success below—first, for life in general, and second, for another area of your life. This can relate to work, home, parenting, or an activity you love.

MY DEFINITION OF SUCCESS IN LIFE

....

....

....

....

MY DEFINITION OF SUCCESS IN

....

....

....

....

To this day, I still turn to these definitions when a big personal or professional decision is hanging in the balance. Putting pen to paper is important here because it will help anchor you to your goals.

I believe the ripple effect of how we define success can be seen and felt by others, especially in our professional lives. When I was collecting titles and trophies, I was unknowingly sending a signal to all the women who worked for me that winning was all that mattered. Fast-forward to today, and if you asked anyone who works for me, they would tell you that impacting the lives of other women is what makes the world go 'round for me. Actions speak louder than words, and every action I take today is in honor of *nobody's* definition of success but my own. In my mind, that's the only way women, moms especially, can "have it all."

When I left my successful advertising career behind to start my business, I focused only on chasing my own definition of success. For me, this included writing love notes to friends, watching my children laugh, and holding my husband's hand. The truth is, it's not that hard to have it all when your definition is based in reality and is all your own.

THE SPARKLE OF SYNCHRONICITY

The final ripple effect you'll experience is a somewhat magical one. I learned that when you find the courage to follow your own North Star, the universe will send you signs of support as if to say "Keep going! You're on the right path!" For example, an ideal new babysitter moves into the neighborhood precisely when you need her most, or a house with built-in bunk beds comes on the market just when you're outgrowing your old home. Some refer to these remarkable events as coincidences, but not me. My experience has taught me that when you make decisions that are in alignment with your true self, a divine intelligence helps bring your desires to fruition.

Spiritual leaders call this phenomenon synchronicity. The first time

I experienced it, it *literally* took my breath away. It happened on a cool winter evening, just after I shared an early version of my coming-out TED Talk with a local Buddhist sangha, long before I had the courage to give the talk on the actual TED stage. During my speech, I explained what it felt like to live in the wreckage of my own doubt, to constantly fear the future, and the irony of being seen as someone at the top of her game while I was actually at rock bottom. I closed by describing how meditation had become my savior, my chance to see and think clearly, and I compared its effects on my life to the Van Morrison lyrics "When that foghorn blows, you know I'll be coming home." After I finished, a woman in the group commented that I looked ten years younger for having shared my truth. And I felt it! When leaving that night, I got in my car and turned on the radio. The same Van Morrison song not only was playing, but it also was cued up to the *exact* same lyrics. That, my friends, was not a coincidence; it was unconditional love, support, and encouragement from something bigger than me saying, "Keep up the good work, lady."

As you start living your life in alignment with what's inside your heart rather than what you see in the world, how will your ripple effect inspire the universe to show up and support you? Keep your eyes and ears peeled, because for me, more often than not, these undeniable signs come in the form of music. For example, the first time I took time away from a business trip in California to hike a mountain trail, at the exact second I reached the peak, the song "Wide Open Spaces" by the Dixie Chicks started playing on my music station. It was a "way to go" from the universe. And when I found myself lying on the bathroom floor mentally drained from pouring my heart into this book, the song

"Don't Stop Believin'" by Journey came on Pandora. I interpreted it as encouragement to get my ass up and keep going.

I'm no longer shocked or surprised when synchronicity shows up, but I'm always in awe. What's important to know is that you're not alone in your journey. As you make both big and small changes in your life, my advice is that instead of looking to friends and family to validate the shifts you're making, look to the universe. According to the women I work with, these signs come in the form of everything—from music, birds, and epic sunsets to unsolicited support from strangers, evening plans canceled when you really were dying to go to bed at 8:30 p.m., or simply the *deeply* held belief that you're doing the right thing.

It's important to know that the universe's support doesn't always come in the form of positive affirmations; sometimes it shows up in the form of flat-out failure. Looking back on my life, I see countless examples of dismissal that turned out to be remarkable blessings in disguise. Thank goodness my dream of attending the University of Virginia was crushed by a rejection letter, because I ended up attending James Madison University and meeting my husband, Richard, the love of my life. And yay for me for having previous versions of this book rejected twenty-six times over four years, because I eventually teamed up with the right agent, editor, and publisher who were *meant* to bring it into the world.

Sometimes the universe will push you forward, and sometimes it will knock you down to see if you get back up. The good news is that just like your intuition knows her shit, so does the universe, because the energy behind them is one and the same. Trust yourself, look for signs that you're on the right path, and watch the ripple effect of self-love change everything.

BE THE *slayer* YOU WANT TO SEE IN THE WORLD.

CHAPTER 14

Raising Dragon Slayers

*W*ith your self-doubt dead and gone, the next step is to ensure your children learn from your dragon-slaying ways by giving them access to the tools and role models they need to slay theirs as well. You know what it's like to be afraid of your own doubts and fears, but did you ever think you could be afraid of your children's as well? If you are, you might be tempted to look the other way when you see your own flesh and blood beating themselves up the same way you once did. Having an open and honest dialogue about dragons will help you resist the temptation to dismiss or deny your kids' worries. It's easy to toss off "It's okay" or "It's not that big a deal" when a child doubts their latest BFF snafu, social status, or ability to make the basketball team. But you don't want your children to feed their half-formed fire-breathers because Mom is too scared to talk about her own. Honesty is the best policy.

In our final chapter, I'll explain how you might not remember exactly what it's like to be made fun of for having buckteeth or for being shorter than everyone else in the class, but you do have recent memories and feelings related to what rejection, alienation, self-doubt, and self-criticism feel like. And you know there's *nothing* like showing the world your true, vulnerable, and imperfect self and feeling proud about doing so. Along those lines, your children need to know that you see them—all of them—including their pain and suffering. This is one of the hardest aspects of being a mother, but it's crucial to show your kids that talking about their problems is better than okay—it's safe, acceptable, and admired in your home. I'll also share some tips on how to resist the urge to solve your children's challenges for them when they're faced with dragons. Children need to feel okay with having problems, and they need to learn how to solve them so they don't feed their dragons. Furthermore, they must learn how to confront the beast each time it tries to surface.

You've come so far—fighting, clawing, and slaying your way to a new you. Don't start doubting yourself now. There's no reason to be intimidated about helping your kids slay their dragons. You found the tools you needed inside you, and it's time to help your children do the same. The greatest gift a mother could give her kids is to reinforce a healthy self-image that empowers them to present themselves to the world with authenticity, strength, and compassion.

TAKE CHARGE, MAMA

In most cultures around the world, men are thought to be the stronger species and therefore the ones who should teach their children how to stand up for themselves, battle for what they believe in, and maybe even throw a right hook when necessary. However, when it comes to slaying dragons, I believe mothers are better equipped to be the role model that kids need because they're more likely to have battled and conquered their own demons. As I noted earlier, most men show up to my workshops unable to conjure up the most recent terrible thing they said to themselves, and even when they do, it sounds something like "Hey, dude, do better next time." I'm not a psychologist, but from my vantage point, men are less likely to argue, fuss, and fight with debilitating self-doubt. I witnessed this phenomenon in full color when my ninety-three-year-old grandfather read one of my blog posts about the mean voice in my head and remarked, "I see what you're saying, Katherine, but I just don't have all that stuff going on in my head. It makes me want to drink a vodka tonic just thinking about it!"

I think it's wonderful that men are wired differently (fewer traffic jams, remember) because the last thing we need is for both Mom *and* Dad to fear the future, lack the courage to say no, and size themselves up against other parents in the neighborhood. There is a lot that women can learn from men in terms of reducing the complexity around our decisions and a lot your children can learn from you, such as how to spot, tame, and slay their own self-doubt. Because you've gone to battle and emerged victorious, you're the perfect person to help your sons and especially your daughters do the same. You're not just a mom who catches the kids before they fall, heals boo-boos with air kisses, and packs love notes in lunch boxes. You're a mom who helps your children confront their deepest fears, annihilate their self-sabotaging behavior, and kick their fire-breathing dragon to the curb.

WHEN PARENTING PUSHES YOUR BUTTONS

My hope is that some of the techniques in this chapter will not only help your children, but also offer you peace of mind. Your past doubts, fears, and insecurities will inevitably show up in your parenting experience, but the good news is that with your dragon dead and gone, you're better equipped to spot scenarios in which its echo can still be heard.

Parenting can be a painful trigger. For example, a stay-at-home mother whose husband left her in a messy divorce might project her loneliness and need for companionship onto her children, and any signs that they're too cool to hang out with her when they're teenagers will feel deeply painful. A working mother who never felt respected for her talent in the office might transfer the responsibility for that old wound to her children by feeling incredibly rejected when they don't clean their plates after she labored over dinner. Irrational responses to very normal events in a family's life cycle are clues you need to look for to see if your dragon's echo is piping up. Do you find yourself losing your mind and ability to use kind words when your daughter leaves two peas on her plate? Does your blood boil when your child misbehaves in public? If your children disobey the rules, do you want to lock them in their rooms for the rest of their lives? If so, get curious in these moments. Hit pause before you scream and yell and see how your child's behavior might mirror or be related to prior wounds.

However, remember that you're no longer the wounded soldier you once were. You've confronted your doubts and insecurities, and in slaying your dragon, you took back control of your thoughts, actions, and happiness. And just as you decided that your former best friend, micromanaging boss, and condescending father were not responsible for your happiness, it's time to realize that your children are not responsible for it either. This will free you from punishing them when they don't deliver the goods. According to parenting coach Suzanne Hanky, kids who are brought into this world with the job to make their parents happy or proud are "emotional mules." When we give children a duty they're not equipped to handle—you know, like anticipating and fulfilling your needs—it results in heightened pressure, stress, and anxiety in both the parents and the children. Demonstrating empathy for what your children are going through and allowing them to self-soothe and solve some of their own problems will send a clear sign that when it comes to happiness, they're responsible for theirs and you're responsible for yours.

START TALKING

As you go about your dragon-free day, don't be afraid to talk to your children about times when you struggled with self-doubt or even instances where you slipped and found yourself momentarily second-guessing your ability to say no or to stay in the present moment. The downside if we mothers don't do this is that we'll unknowingly raise the next generation to be unable to fight the dragons that we don't or can't talk about. Don't sweep these important conversations under the rug because they make you uncomfortable. You can't solve problems if you're unable to talk about them.

One of the most effective ways I've found to embrace your children's mistakes, mishaps, and setbacks is to play the conversation starter I call "Onward and Upward." As you sit around the dinner table, invite each family member to share the one mistake they learned the most from that day. You'll get beyond your children's typical response of "fine" when you ask how their day was, and more importantly, they'll see that their own mother (gasp) makes mistakes too. This process also teaches your children that you love them, and by that, I mean *every bit* of them, mistakes and all. Never forget that in a young child's eyes, love and approval are the same thing. They need to know, trust, and believe that their parents don't just love the good stuff.

Another ripple effect of having open and vulnerable exchanges is that kids learn to self-correct when they come to believe they could be doing better. For example, when I first started doing the prior exercise with my kids, my son often said that his biggest mistake was staying in bed too long in the morning after his alarm went off, causing him to be rushed and stressed when getting ready for school. After he shared that same mistake two days in a row, on the third day, I noticed that he got out of bed faster and easier. I'm not suggesting he was happy about it—there was a lot of moaning—but by recognizing and admitting his role in the process, he took control of the situation without being asked. It turned into a great lesson in living, learning, and taking responsibility for actions—at eight years old, no less!

KNOWING WHEN TO SHUT UP AND LISTEN

I didn't acquire the coping mechanisms for dealing with the highs and lows of life until I was thirty-five, when I forced myself through a self-imposed, self-help journey. So just imagine the *gift* you'll be giving your children by teaching them that everyone doubts themselves, but those doubts don't have to be all-consuming or debilitating. To help your kids stop their own dragons from flourishing, your little ones need empathy. Let's look at an example from Ellie, a mother of eight-year-old twins, who attended one of my workshops. During the session, Ellie shared that when her daughter Lila would come home from school upset that the other kids had made fun of her because her hair was short and wispy instead of long and flowing, or that she felt panicked about her upcoming science test, Ellie's first instinct was to say, "Don't worry, sweetie. Everyone has different hair, and you don't need to be stressed about your grades at this age. Everything will be okay." While this may have worked on some children, it didn't work on Lila. Yet Ellie continued deploying this tactic until she realized during one of my workshops that while she had feared her own self-doubt for years, she was flat-out terrified of her daughter's, and that's why she was unknowingly shutting those conversations down. She was allowing her own dragon to tag team with Lila's, which trained her daughter to groom her own fears and doubts.

We talked about how Ellie could change her approach by listening to her daughter instead of negating Lila's doubt by brushing it under the carpet. Ellie decided that the next time it happened, she'd validate her daughter's worries and bring them into the open. Rather than tell her daughter to be quiet, she'd ask her daughter to tell her more. When the kids nagged Lila again, Ellie asked heartfelt questions: "How does it make you feel when they say that about your hair? Do you know we have the same hair, and people made fun of me when I was a little girl?" "Tell me about this science test of yours. Is it going to be super hard? I was never really good at science either, you know." As a result, Ellie's relationship with her daughter changed. Lila learned it was okay to have doubts, fears, and anxieties but not to let them get the best of her. And Ellie learned that honesty, vulnerability, and imperfection were far more beneficial to *both* of them than pretending dragons didn't exist at all.

If you want to put this principle into practice, try this activity. The next time your child is upset about an upcoming book report or getting picked last for the dodgeball team, resist the temptation to say

"It's okay" and keep making the lasagna. Put the noodles down and say, "That really stinks, honey. I'd be upset too. What do you need me to know?" It won't be easy, as you're a busy woman with sixty-five things on your to-do list before bedtime, and you might think the last thing you need on a busy night is a bunch of small talk, but give it a whirl. I think you'll be pleasantly surprised with what you learn about yourself and your child along the way.

Remember that dragons thrive in the land of silence, darkness, and avoidance. Therefore, the most courageous thing you can do is let your children battle their dragon out loud—to struggle and experience adversity beyond their own minds. Furthermore, don't assume that expressing empathy is important only when you have young children. As Susan Engel, a mother of two, pointed out in the powerful November 28, 2012, *New York Times* article "When They're Grown, the Real Pain Begins," being open to her children's challenges when they were little came easy. This changed, however, when her son grew up, was injured in an accident, faced a romantic split that broke his heart, and dealt with a boss who fired him without warning or rationale. Longing to solve all his problems, but unable to do so, Engel assumed she just wasn't cut out to be the parent of adult children. But just as she was having heart palpitations and feeling sick over how to help, her grown son confronted her. "Mom," he said, "when I tell you what's wrong, I don't want you to tell me how to fix it, and I don't want you to tell me it's not as bad as I think. I just want your sympathy." Stunned into silence, Susan thought to herself, *Sympathy? That's all he needs? I can do that.*

People often think of empathy as trying to walk in someone else's shoes and feel what they're feeling. But it's actually about saying,

"I think I understand how this feels to you, and you're not alone." Responding with empathy means finding a way to tell your children that their feelings make sense, they have a right to feel the way they do, and you're not there to shut their feelings down. I always tell mothers that if getting into this headspace feels hard, just think how you feel when you confide in your husband that you think the PTA president is out to get you, and without even processing the possibility, he reduces your very real fear to dust by saying, "Don't be ridiculous." It sucks, right? Well, that's exactly how your daughter feels when she says the same about her sixth-grade teacher and you tell her it's all in her head and quickly get back to burning the brussels sprouts. Don't bolt when your children express self-doubt. Odds are they don't want you to solve their problems for them (just like you don't want the men in your life to solve yours). They simply need a safe environment to process their fears without feeling ashamed for having them.

LETTING CHILDREN SOLVE THEIR OWN PROBLEMS

It seems that moms are born with the desire to help, heal, and make all their children's problems go away. Call it maternal instinct, unconditional empathy, or hurry up and help, but it seems to be part of our hardwiring from the very beginning. In fact, a team of researchers at the Eunice Kennedy Shriver National Institute of Child Health and Human Development set out to explore the brain patterns involved in maternal responses to the sound of infants crying. The researchers analyzed the behavior of 684 mothers across eleven countries and found that on average, mothers picked up, held, and talked to their children within five seconds of hearing them cry. Even while enclosed in an MRI scanner with no baby in sight, when mothers listened to the sound of an infant crying versus other sounds, researchers could detect enhanced activity in brain territories linked to the intention to move and speak. In other words, our first instinct when a child needs help is to jump into action.

When you're looking to raise strong, resilient, and dragon-proof children, one of the greatest gifts you can give them, according to Hanky, is the opportunity to solve some of their own problems. She says that if you do all the hard work for your children—prodding them along to take bite after bite at the dinner table, hovering over them as they complete their math facts, or putting words in their mouth about how to handle every social injustice at school—they never develop the abilities or the confidence to figure problems out on their own, potentially increasing their self-doubt and dependence on others. She says there are two simple and crucial ways that moms can empower their kids with confidence and self-compassion and ensure that it comes from internal rather than external sources. The first is to avoid turning your children's problems into your problems. For example, let's say your son hates broccoli, but that's what you're serving for dinner tonight. If you spend the entire meal saying things like "Please take another bite," "Okay, three more bites and you can be done," or "If you eat two more bites, you can have ice cream for dessert," you've instantly made his problem your problem. Funny how that works.

Hanky's advice is simple on this front. When you see your child's knees going weak or fake tears pouring out of their eyes, think to yourself, *This is not my problem to solve.* On the dinner front (which, if you'll recall, is the number one pain point of mothers around the world), the solution isn't complicated. Take a deep breath and say, "It's tough to eat things you're not crazy about. Tonight, we have broccoli. Not your favorite, I know. You can eat it and enjoy our dinner together or not and excuse yourself to your room. Either is fine." According to Hanky, kids are free to not like broccoli, free to not eat broccoli, but they can't sit around and complain about broccoli. The key here is that the child is in charge of the decision, not you. Kids never feel in charge because grown-ups boss them around all day, every day—it's an overwhelming and unempowering experience. By giving your children the option to decide whether to eat the meal, you're teaching them key decision-making skills and that other people don't always get to decide what's best for them—which will serve them well later in life.

I recently deployed this decision-making technique on my daughter after she got the tips of her hair dyed red at the hairdresser and then refused to take a shower that same day for fear of her fabulous new look fading. Hanky taught me the power of deploying empathy and then forced decision-making. I said, "I can see why you'd be worried about your hair. I would feel exactly the same way. However, getting clean before school tomorrow is not negotiable, so how can you adhere to the rules while also protecting what's important to you?" Without much thought, she quickly came up with three options: wear a shower cap in the shower, opt for a bath instead, or take a shower the next morning to let the color set in a bit longer. It worked like magic, and along the way, it taught my daughter that she doesn't have to be backed into a corner by others and do as they say; she's creative and smart enough to determine how to say yes on her own terms.

Another way to teach your children to doubt themselves less and trust their instincts more is to think of yourself as their coach and not their mommy during challenging times. According to Hanky, when kids don't follow the rules, mothers tend to take it *very* personally. When your toddler falls apart at the grocery store, you might think or even say, "Get up! You're embarrassing me!" Or when your daughter runs late for the bus in the morning, you worry the bus driver will think *you* don't have your act together. Interestingly, while mothers worry about their children's actions being a reflection of themselves, which activates their authoritarian mode, coaches are committed to skill development and working as a team to achieve the desired outcome. If a baseball player turns in a pitiful performance, his coach's job is to understand what happened and help him develop the skills to avoid the scenario in the future.

To use the case of your daughter who regularly runs late for the bus, take off your mommy hat, sit her down, and allow *her* to come up with several ways to prevent the morning panic. I know it's faster to tell your children what to do, but their own problem-solving skills might surprise you. Even if they only come up with one solution, that's winning! Remember that your job as a mother is not to push, poke, and prod your children into being perfect specimens who are always on time, forever polite, and incapable of saying anything even slightly annoying. Your job is to help your children understand they're human, learn coping mechanisms, and develop sustainable self-esteem. I think you'll also find that you will yell, scream, and roll your eyes at your children less often when you acknowledge your role as their coach instead of drill sergeant.

KEEP DOING WHAT YOU'RE DOING. THEY'RE WATCHING.

One surefire way to tame your children's insecurities is to make sure yours are tamed as well. The idea that your children are watching and learning from your behavior might be a horrifying concept because sometimes you yell at your son to stop yelling at his sister, you work through entire beach vacations, and you drink wine out of a box for easy access. But as you know, children are like sponges—absorbing everything we do as parents. And it's not just the bad stuff they're picking up. It's the good stuff too. When you say no to your boss to attend a field trip with your son, he's paying attention to your priorities; when you look in the mirror and like what you see rather than cursing yourself under your breath, your daughter is learning how to look in the mirror as well; and when you make a mistake and say you're sorry, everyone in your house learns that mishaps are accepted and apologies are awesome. Kristen, a mother who attended one of my workshops, elaborated on the ripple effect of saying "I'm sorry" in her house—the more she said it, the more she witnessed her children saying it to friends, neighbors, teachers, and people in the checkout line at the grocery store. To me, the real power of saying "I'm sorry" is less about apologizing for a mistake and more about the recognition and admission that you made one in the first place.

Apologies are infectious, and so is perfectionism. In her 2012 book *Daring Greatly*, Brené Brown says, "I'm convinced perfectionism is actually contagious. If we struggle with being, living, and looking absolutely perfect, we might as well line our children up and slip those little perfection straitjackets over their heads." I personally felt the backlash of this phenomenon several years ago when I called a parenting coach for advice because I was unsure how to handle my daughter's reaction to her own report card. Despite the fact that she received straight A's, the results weren't satisfying enough because, as she pointed out, "All the tests, quizzes, and homework assignments that went into those final grades were not also A's." In other words, she felt she received grades that she didn't fully deserve or earn, no matter what her report card said. What was the first thing the parenting coach said to me? "Tell me what examples of perfectionism your daughter is seeing at home." Let's just say I hung up the phone and drove straight to her office.

Just as it would be challenging to teach your children to be a great cook when you only know how to use the microwave, or how to play basketball when you can't even dribble, you can't teach your children to be a better dragon slayer than you are. So, keep on keeping on. Remain steadfast in shutting down any shadow of a doubt that you're not worthy of self-love and support, and you'll be showing your children that they're not only worthy of your love, but also their own. At the end of the day, you must be what you want your children to become. I love it when Brown says, "Who we are and how we carry ourselves are stronger predictors of how our children will turn out than what we know about parenting." In that sense, one of your primary responsibilities as a parent isn't to love your children more, but to love yourself more.

EPILOGUE

Slay On

"I HAVE MET MY SELF AND I AM GOING
TO CARE FOR HER FIERCELY."

—GLENNON DOYLE MELTON

*T*he strength and courage you've developed to confront and defeat your self-doubt is an incredible triumph. You should feel immensely braver, stronger, and more resilient than when you first cracked open this book. But always remember that the true weight, magnitude, and monumental relief that come from slaying your dragon will only ever be felt by you. Others may never say "Good job, you!" or "Way to take down that dark, evil force that was holding you back!" Because they've never felt your pain, they'll never understand the life-changing relief that comes from eliminating it. The other day, I asked my husband what he felt was the greatest change in me since I slayed my dragon. He said, "Honestly, I don't think the people around you would say there's been a dramatic change—you're still the bubbly, successful, smart woman you've always been. The difference has been how you see yourself internally—people always loved and respected you, but now you finally love and respect yourself."

And that's what it all comes down to, my friend. While there's certainly a lot of pomp and circumstance, soul-searching, battle cries, mantras, and messy experiences associated with slaying your dragon, at the end of the day, you're simply killing the warped self-image you once carried around like a backpack full of dead weight. With the burden of that fictitious baggage gone, the way you see yourself will finally catch up to the way others have *always* seen you—as a beautiful, bright, and capable human being. Eventually, your newfound self-acceptance and love will eclipse any need for external approval, and your opinion of yourself will be the only one that matters.

Slaying dragons isn't easy, but it's the greatest gift you could ever give yourself, your family, and your children. In so many ways, you're giving birth to a new you. Author and spiritual teacher Iyanla Vanzant once said, "The life you want is just on the other side of the labor pains it will take to birth it." Nobody ever said bursting forth a new life was easy—all that sweating and pushing and grunting can wear a girl down—but the end result? It's oh so worth it.

Eradicating your self-doubt is a fight worth fighting because *you* are worth winning. No matter what your children, partner, boss, or best friend throw your way, never forget that your beautiful soul is worthy of the happiness, inner peace, and freedom you've worked so hard to achieve. When challenging times rain down, and they will, it helps to harness all you have by remembering that you're not alone in this battle like you once assumed you were. The dragon slayer in me sees, honors, and respects the dragon slayer in you. In fact, there's a whole sisterhood of us out there, and it's growing. We're fighting the good fight and living to tell about it. And now, just like me, you're blazing a trail for others to follow because every time a mother slays her dragon of self-doubt, she sharpens the sword for another woman to do the same.

Embrace the warrior you've become and revel in the freedom you feel today, but never stop learning, growing, and finding new ways to love yourself. After all, you didn't come this far only to get this far.

Keep slaying.

INTERESTED IN MORE
SELF-HELP RESOURCES?

My favorite self-help books:

* ✸ *Finding Your Own North Star: Claiming the Life You Were Meant to Live* by Martha Beck (Three Rivers Press, 2001).

* ✸ *The Power of Now: A Guide to Spiritual Enlightenment* by Eckhart Tolle (Namaste Publishing, 1997).

* ✸ *Spirit Junkie: A Radical Road to Self-Love and Miracles* by Gabrielle Bernstein (Three Rivers Press, 2011).

* ✸ *The Untethered Soul* by Michael A. Singer (New Harbinger Publications, 2007).

* ✸ *Within: A Spiritual Awakening to Love & Weight Loss* by Dr. Habib Sadeghi (Open Road Media, 2014).

* ✸ *Women, Food, and God: The Unexpected Path to Almost Everything* by Geneen Roth (Scribner, 2016).

My life coach: fogdogcoaching.com

Devin helps professionals, healers, entrepreneurs, and leaders who feel restless or stuck to find clarity in their circumstances and to understand, own, and communicate their truths, their gifts, and their paths forward. Her approach is intuitive, supportive, quick, and effective. She gets right to the heart of her clients and guides them forward on their true path.

INTERESTED IN LEARNING FROM LIKE-MINDED MOTHERS?

Visit slaylikeamother.com or follow @slaylikeamother on Instagram to learn from other dragon-slaying mothers. Motherhood is hard—the more we open up and share, the more we pave the way for other women to do the same.

WANT TO KEEP SLAYING?

Download a PDF from slaylikeamother.com that features each of the exercises from the book, as well as a master "Slaying Schematic" that will help you encapsulate your dragon-slaying ways in one place.

Acknowledgments

To everyone who helped this dream come true. My ever-loving gratitude goes to...

My parents, Bob and Nancy. For loving me, for believing in me even when I didn't believe in myself, for demonstrating that hard work and perseverance make anything possible, and for trusting me to share my broken bits with the world in an effort to help other women, mothers, and young girls do the same.

My brother, Chris. For showing me what it means to dedicate your life to helping others, for driving home from college to comfort me when I needed you most, and for letting me talk your ear off for hours as I came to terms with my personal journey.

My husband, Richard. For loving me unconditionally, for leaving your life in Switzerland to start a new one in America, and for being the greatest friend, husband, and father a girl could ask for. Thank you for carrying a heavy load at home so I could pour my heart into these pages. I used to think I didn't deserve to be with someone so amazing, but I finally believe I do.

My daughter, Layla. For inspiring me to tell my story. I hope that watching your mother slay her dragon will give you the courage to never allow one to enter your own life. Girls can do tough things, and you're the toughest girl I know. And thank you for pimping my book to the local library in hopes that they carry it. I'll never forget that as long as I live.

My son, Alex. For letting me snuggle with your teddies, for constantly telling me you love me "google times google times infinity," and for proclaiming that you'll be the very first person to buy this book. You're the sweetest guy I know, and I love you google times google times infinity right back.

My father-in-law, Ronnie. For being the first Wintsch to have your name on the cover of a book and inspiring me to follow in your footsteps. Oh, how I wish you were here to see it.

My mother-in-law, Liz. For always reading my blog, sending rave reviews, and proving that the insights I had to share were not unique to young mothers in America but even wise grandmothers in Switzerland!

My partner in crime, Kristina. For believing women would benefit from this message, introducing me to an amazing agent, and teaching me how to write a book while holding my hand and heartache along the way.

My agent, Daniel. For taking a chance on a first-time author, for coming up with the dragon-slaying theme that changed everything, and for not allowing this book to be an anthology.

My editor, Shana, and the team at Sourcebooks. For saying yes, for penning the greatest offer letter ever written, for cheering me on when I needed it most, and for putting hard-earned money on the line to make this dream a reality.

My research assistant, Lauren. For scouring the world of scientific and academic research and serving up the right studies at the right time to add weight and credibility to the struggles mothers face around the world. And for loving sloths so much.

My self-help support system, Alex. For reading worn-out copies of my favorite self-help books and meticulously transferring circled paragraphs, OMG moments, and messy margin notes into a usable format. I'm sure you learned more about me than you ever wanted to know.

My business partner, Lauren. For running The Mom Complex single-handedly and wholeheartedly for two years so I could give birth to this book. You took the company, your impact, and our PB&J relationship to a whole new level. And, of course, for saying "like a mother" after I said "slay" in what turned out to be the best book title ever. Oh, and for telling me to put on my sunglasses when ugly crying in public.

My Mom Complex warrior, Emma. For always making me laugh, for keeping my first dream (The Mom Complex) alive so I could bring a second one (this book) to life. And for teaching me that the punctuation almost *always* goes inside the quotation marks. I somehow made it through my entire life without knowing that.

My friend, Jamie. For pushing me to write blog posts more frequently, booking major speaking engagements, and providing invaluable feedback to strengthen my message to moms.

To my former boss, Earl. For filling my soul with valuable life lessons, teaching me how to let go, and providing unconditional love when I needed it most.

My friend, Kate. For showing up on a yellow bicycle at my office and being the first person who believed this story could be a book.

My trustworthy Microsoft Word. For never crashing, spinning out of control, or losing *any* content from the manuscript. And for not judging me as you corrected thousands of words I cannot spell.

My dragon. For teaching me that I'm lovelier, stronger, and braver than I ever knew.

About the Author

Katherine Wintsch is an internationally recognized expert on the topic of modern motherhood. The majority of her expertise comes from studying the passion and pain points of mothers around the world the rest is accumulated from a little trial and a whole lot of error while raising her own two children with her husband, Richard, in Richmond, Virginia.

Photo credit: Dean Whitbeck

As the founder and CEO of The Mom Complex, Katherine and her team help develop innovative new products, services, and marketing strategies for the world's largest mom-focused brands. Companies get better bottom lines and moms get better lives— what's not to love?

Although she loves her innovation work, Katherine's true passion is directly impacting the lives of mothers, which she does through her writing, public speaking, and dragon-slaying workshops. She is known for having audiences crying one minute and laughing the next. Attending one of her workshops is always a life-changing experience.

Katherine's sought-after research and expertise have been featured by the *Today* show, the *New York Times*, the *Wall Street Journal*, and Fast Company, and she regularly writes about the topic of motherhood on her popular blog *Slay Like a Mother*, as well as for *Huffington Post* and *Working Mother* magazine. When she's not helping other mothers find inner peace, you can find her shopping with her daughter, snuggling with her son, vacationing with her husband, or meditating first thing in the morning before the house wakes up and turns to complete chaos.